On Education, Formation, Citizenship and the Lost Purpose of Learning

Reading Augustine

Series Editor:
Miles Hollingworth

Reading Augustine offers personal and close readings of
St. Augustine of Hippo from leading philosophers and religious
scholars. Its aim is to make clear Augustine's importance to
contemporary thought and to present Augustine not only or
primarily as a pre-eminent Christian thinker but as a philosophical,
spiritual, literary, and intellectual icon of the West.

Volumes in the series:
On Ethics, Politics and Psychology in the Twenty-First Century
John Rist
On Love, Confession, Surrender and the Moral Self
Ian Clausen
*On Education, Formation, Citizenship and the Lost Purpose
of Learning*
Joseph Clair
On Creativity, Liberty, Love and the Beauty of the Law
Todd Breyfogle
*On Consumer Culture, Identity, The Church and the Rhetorics
of Delight* (forthcoming)
Mark Clavier
On Self-Harm, Narcissism, Atonement and the Vulnerable Christ
(forthcoming)
David Vincent Meconi
On God, The Soul, Evil and the Rise of Christianity (forthcoming)
John Peter Kenney
On Music, Sound, Affect and Ineffability (forthcoming)
Carol Harrison

On Education, Formation, Citizenship and the Lost Purpose of Learning

Joseph Clair

Bloomsbury Academic
An imprint of Bloomsbury Publishing Inc

B L O O M S B U R Y
NEW YORK • LONDON • OXFORD • NEW DELHI • SYDNEY

Bloomsbury Academic

An imprint of Bloomsbury Publishing Inc

1385 Broadway	50 Bedford Square
New York	London
NY 10018	WC1B 3DP
USA	UK

www.bloomsbury.com

BLOOMSBURY and the Diana logo are trademarks of Bloomsbury Publishing Plc

First published 2018

© Joseph Clair, 2018

Library of Congress Cataloging-in-Publication Data

A catalog record for this book is available from the Library of Congress.

ISBN:	HB:	978-1-5013-2615-8
	PB:	978-1-5013-2616-5
	ePub:	978-1-5013-2617-2
	ePDF:	978-1-5013-2618-9

Series: Reading Augustine

Cover design: Catherine Wood
Cover image © Pan Xunbin/Shutterstock

Typeset by Integra Software Services Pvt. Ltd.
Printed and bound in the United States of America

To find out more about our authors and books visit www.bloomsbury.com. Here you will find extracts, author interviews, details of forthcoming events, and the option to sign up for our newsletters.

For the Students of the
William Penn Honors Program

Contents

Acknowledgments

I've had the opportunity to study in many different educational institutions—a large state university, a Christian liberal arts college, a private research university, a Jesuit institution, one of the original medieval universities, and the American ivy league—before landing my first job at an evangelical Quaker liberal arts college in the Pacific Northwest. I was hired to launch the honors curriculum—a challenge which has given me the opportunity to consider the deepest purpose of learning and the moral and spiritual formation that might accompany it.

In my considerations, Augustine of Hippo has been my greatest conversation partner. As master educator, the great bishop gave many of his best thoughts to these questions and this book is a record of our conversation. From Augustine I have learned that education is a gift—not given for self-indulgence or pride, but for the sake of God and others. It teaches us to care about the right sorts of things, and to put our lives to good use.

The William Penn Honors Program at George Fox University is an experiment in this kind of Christian education. To the extraordinary team of teachers, administrators, and friends—Abigail Favale, Javier Garcia, Jane Sweet, Jocelyn Stein, Brian Doak, Mark Hall, Corwynn Beals, Caitlin Corning, Leah Payne, Roger Nam, Paul Otto, Bill Jolliff, Robin Baker, Rob Westervelt, and Linda Samek—thanks for your camaraderie in realizing the dream thus far.

To the people who helped shape, inspire, and enable this book— especially Adam Eitel, Tim Roth, mentor and coach, Todd Breyfogle, friend of a lifetime and super-editor, Andrew Henscheid, my kids, August, Esme, and Maggie, dad and friend, Allan, mom and friend, Mary Ann, and before, after, and above all, Nora—thank you.

To Miles Hollingworth, whose keen mind drew this book out of me, to Haaris Naqvi and Katherine De Chant for expert editorial guidance at Bloomsbury, and to Rajesh Kathamuthu for cheerful assistance, thank you.

To the many extraordinary teachers who shaped me—John Wagner, Alice Ann Eberman, and Bob Webber, to name a few—without you I would never have learned to love learning nor grasped its innate connection to love for God.

To Christ the teacher, the target of true learning, the incomparable designer and Incarnate redeemer of all that is, the Word made flesh: thank you for making this flesh and for giving me these words.

To the extraordinary students of the William Penn Honors Program who taught me how to be a teacher, to you I dedicate this book.

List of Abbreviations

I have used the following English translations of the works of Augustine. The following abbreviations are used to cite the works in the text.

CT   *On Christian Teaching*, trans. R.P.H. Green (New York: Oxford University Press, 1997)

CG   *The City of God*, trans. R.W. Dyson (New York: Cambridge University Press, 1998)

CF   *The Confessions*, trans. Maria Boulding (New York: Vintage Books, 1998)

EP   *Expositions of the Psalms*, trans. Maria Boulding (Hyde Park, NY: New City Press, 2000)

HFJ   *Homilies on the First Epistle of John*, trans. Boniface Ramsey (Hyde Park, NY: New City Press, 2008)

L   *Letters*, trans. Roland Teske, vols. 1–4 (Hyde Park, NY: New City Press, 2001–2005)

OD   *On Order*, trans. Silvano Borruso (South Bend, IN: St. Augustine's Press, 2007)

R   *Revisions*, trans. Boniface Ramsey (Hyde Park, NY: New City Press, 2010).

S   *Sermons*, trans. Edmund Hill, vols. 1–11 (Hyde Park, NY: New City Press, 1990–1997)

T   *The Trinity*, trans. Edmund Hill (Hyde Park, NY: New City Press, 1991)

1

The Lost Purpose of Learning

The apparent problem facing higher education

College is a rich part of the Western cultural imagination and a canonized plot line in the American middle-class mythos. Although it is costly and time-intensive, there are good reasons to be proud of this tradition and to go away for four years to become adults. After all, college leaves an indelible stamp on the soul: the formative lessons of newfound independence, hard work, and leisure in preparation for the business of life. Few institutions have more nostalgic and patriotic bonds of affection that last as long—and procure as many donations—as college and university alumni associations. Americans talk and think about college all the time. Americans eagerly read the *U.S. News & World Report*'s college rankings—despite criticisms about its validity—as a way of dreaming of the future and measuring oneself against the world. Many Americans begin saving when their children are born. Many stay up late worrying about their kindergartener's grades and violin lessons. Many spend thousands of dollars on college prep tests and campus visits for their high schoolers.

But is it worth it? What is college? Contrary to the popular image of the exhausted student amidst a pile of books, recent reports by the U.S. Bureau of Labor Statistics reveal that the average college student only spends 3.5 hours a day on educational activities (a combination of class and study hours) compared to the 4.0 hours of leisure and sports activities and 8.8 hours of sleep. Lest one think this is because all college students work three jobs and pay their own way through school, the study also reveals that students spend 2.3 hours a day on average at non-college-related jobs. Not only do students give significant fractions of time to a variety of endeavors, but they seem unsure about what to do with their primary purpose of being in college. According to the National Center for Education Statistics (NCES), 80 percent of students change their major at least once; and for those who do change it, they do so, on average, at least three times.

After the recession of 2008, the value of college education itself seems to be hanging in the balance. For the fifth straight year college enrollment is down. Fall term enrollment this academic year (2016–17) in the United States dipped by 1.4 percent to 19.01 million students according to the National Student Clearinghouse Research Center. This decline represents a 1.59-million student decrease from the 20.6-million enrollment peak in 2011. Part of this dip may represent a decline in adult students (over the age of 24) who are increasingly interested in ditching the degree in favor of a job. Yet in *The Atlantic* last year, Alia Wong pointed out that this trend also continues a widening gap between high school graduation and college enrollment in this country: In 2013–14, 82 percent of high school seniors made it to graduation (an all-time high), yet only 66 percent immediately enrolled in college (down from 69 percent in 2008).[1]

One plausible explanation for the decline in enrollment is the skyrocketing cost of college tuition and the resulting student debt. The average cost of tuition at private colleges in 2016–17 was $33,480, and in 2015, 68 percent of college seniors graduated with an average of $30,100 in debt, a number that has been steadily climbing over the past ten years. The reasons for the cost spike are multiple—new student services, amenities, sports programs, etc.—many of which have to do with increasing competition for the sacred but slimming

---

[1] https://www.theatlantic.com/education/archive/2016/01/where-are-all-the-high-school-grads-going/423285/ (accessed January 11, 2016).

pool of applicants who are both academic high-achievers and well-to-do—in other words, excellent students whose families can pay their way. This contest and associated cost spike is what is referred to as the "brand new rock climbing wall in the student center" phenomenon in the new college admissions hustle.

Colleges and universities are increasingly sensitive to the cost spike and debt overload. In their effort to control costs, many schools have begun closing "ancillary" departments (mostly in the humanities) and focusing on professional programs (e.g., nursing, engineering, education)—those easiest to connect degree with salary. Some traditional liberal arts colleges have had to close their doors. It amounts to a veritable shake down of traditional liberal arts education in the United States. The causes underlying the maze of statistics are still unclear—a befuddling mix of data that leaves social scientists and educators to forever search for the real causes of the college enrollment decline. It is time to ask more incisive questions. What is a liberal arts education for? Has the traditional four-year liberal arts college or university experience become a rote cultural practice, emptied of significance and value—a ritual for which the original motivating reasons cannot be recalled? Why go to college at all?

The real problem facing higher education

The problem facing higher education is tied to the inability to provide an account of the value of a traditional liberal arts education—the value of college itself—apart from very narrowed economic considerations related to career success, expected incomes, and paychecks. When one asks the question of the value of a college education purely in economic terms—of cost in relation to financial return—the account of the overarching purposes of a college education is restricted to the singularly instrumental question: What will I make?

The liberal arts tradition, out of which American colleges and universities have grown, includes a robust set of answers to the question of the value of a college education that can be boiled down to four essential categories of purpose: intellectual, economic, moral, and spiritual. Today, the intellectual purpose of a college education—expressed in the question: What should I know?—is subordinate to the purely economic, perpetually trying to define and justify itself by its instrumental value, answering the question: What will I make? This approach gives the impression that if one can conceive a relationship between the intellectual purpose and the economic purpose, then college's existence is justified and there is no longer any need to think about the second two purposes—the moral and spiritual—which are increasingly difficult to discuss in a secular and pluralistic society.

Yet today, just as the economic purpose has triumphed, the intellectual purpose of college and university life has been called into question. As Richard Arum and Josipa Roksa persuasively demonstrate in their landmark work, *Academically Adrift: Limited Learning on College Campuses* (University of Chicago, 2010), a disproportionately large percentage of students (over 45 percent in their studies) demonstrate no significant improvement in a range of core skills for which they are ostensibly being trained (e.g., critical thinking, communication) across their four years of education. Their studies suggest that the intellectual purpose of a liberal arts education needs to be ordered toward something other, something higher—perhaps toward the noninstrumental values and goods traditionally associated with liberal arts education—in order to retain its vigor. If the intellectual is ordered solely toward the economic—that is, if education is reduced to utter instrumentality—it will die. The intellectual purpose of a liberal arts college requires a balance between the materially, instrumentally, and economically *useful* on the one hand and the morally and spiritually *praiseworthy* on the other. The intellectual purpose of college is unstable on its own. It needs an aim beyond itself to justify the costs of time and leisure necessary for study. And the economic purpose alone is insufficient to sustain the intellectual enterprise over the long haul. Or so the current cultural crisis over the values of a college education seems to suggest.

Studies generally support the idea that the economic purpose of college remains real—the U.S. Department of Education College Scorecard Web site boasts that college graduates earn, on average, $1 million more than high school graduates over their lifetime. Such details and justifications are of course complex when one takes all the factors—tuition cost, student debt, university alumni salaries, etc.—into account. Take, for example, the 2015 study published by the *Wall Street Journal* that revealed that college graduates (ages 25–29) in the science, technology, engineering, and mathematics related (STEM) disciplines earn on average $76,000 a year compared with humanities majors who earn only $51,000 a year. If the sense of the value of a college education is purely economic and it can be proven that one would be able to make more than $51,000 a year as a young adult, is this a good reason not to go to college and study philosophy? To let one's sense of the value of a college education be exhausted by paychecks is to allow the economic (What will I make?) lead the intellectual (What should I know?). This cultural conversation reveals how deep the economic instrumentalization of education has gone, and it is not merely a matter of the modes by which one goes about justifying college tuition. It has to do with a culture's deepest values—the ones that are implicitly inculcated in students long before they get to college. According to the traditional models of liberal arts education—the ones that gave rise to the modern college and university—to let the economic purpose lead the intellectual is to shape students who navigate knowledge without a North Star. It is to form students who have knowledge and technical mastery over the world without adequately training them in what to do and who to serve with that knowledge and mastery.

To answer the question of the value of a college degree purely in economic terms is to have already lost the battle. In the age of information delivery, online courses, flipped classrooms, and digital fluency, there are already cheaper and shorter routes for career preparation, especially in the lucrative STEM subjects—routes that do not require the onerous and lengthy residential requirements and core curricula found in traditional liberal arts colleges.

Take, for example, the Thiel Fellowship—founded by technology entrepreneur and investor Peter Thiel in 2011. This two-year program offers young people willing to skip college a scholarship of $100,000, a broad professional network of supporters, and a chance to "build new things," things they actually "care about." This fellowship presupposes that, in general, eighteen-year-olds care about the right things and know what the world needs. The Thiel Fellowship should be applauded because it merely makes explicit the instrumentalist view of higher education prevalent today—a view aimed at practical efficiency and lucrative life outcomes. This approach to education dispatches once and for all the stuffy questions: What kinds of people ought colleges aim to form? Who or what ought to be worshiped as the culmination of true learning? These questions of moral and spiritual purpose feel increasingly irrelevant and out of date in liberal education.

The contemporary conversation about the value of a college education reveals all that one needs to know about the crisis—there is no shared language to speak about the moral or spiritual purposes of learning. Western culture is strangely mute about how these purposes relate to economic value and their relevance to the decision to attend, fund, or reform contemporary institutions. This silence about the moral and spiritual purposes of learning reveals a shared confusion about the true nature of education.

A brief history of the soul of education

As mentioned above, the liberal arts tradition out of which American colleges and universities have grown includes a fourfold set of purposes for education: intellectual, economic, moral, and spiritual. For the most significant thinkers in this tradition, the intellectual purpose (What should I know?) and the economic (What shall I make?) are only intelligible in light of, and should be guided by, the moral (What should I do?) and the spiritual (Who or what should I worship?). The latter two purposes—the moral and the spiritual—and their corresponding questions form what I call the soul of liberal arts education. A brief history of this soul reveals three distinct phases or stages—the Platonic in the classical period, the Augustinian Christian in the medieval and early modern periods, and the Romantic in the modern era. Each movement synthesizes the four purposes of learning and attempts to establish the moral and spiritual purposes as the signposts that guide the intellectual craft and economic outcomes of a liberal arts education in a specific historical moment and cultural context.

The moral and spiritual purpose of liberal arts education was born in ancient Greece in Socrates' view of the human being as naturally ordered to pursue truth and to flourish in a learning community. This view was then extended and adapted by Plato and Aristotle in the formation of the liberal arts as a discrete set of disciplines or fields of inquiry to be pursued in formal schools. The seven classical liberal arts—forged in Rome and sharpened in the early Middle Ages— were divided between the trivium (grammar, logic, and rhetoric) and the quadrivium (arithmetic, music, geometry, and astronomy). The trivium focused on the language arts—the relationship between language and reality—and the quadrivium focused on quantity in all of its stunning diversity in the material world. These foundational subjects branch into the many disciplines or fields of inquiry systematized by ancients like Aristotle—including subjects such as philosophy and the natural sciences. Thus the liberal arts were seen as the foundation of the many disciplines that we now think of as the different departments in a college or university. Indeed, accrediting bodies for colleges and universities still require broad training in the seven liberal arts as partial requirements for graduation. These arts—not merely the fine arts—were labeled *liberal* in the ancient world because they were preparation for being a good citizen—a *liber* in Latin—a "free person" worthy to participate in a self-governing society. They stand in contrast to the servile or mechanical arts aimed solely at manual training in practical crafts. This view of education entails a substantive view of human nature, in which development in the "liberal" modes of learning accords with our essence as creatures and provides the intellectual and moral formation for a good life and a good society.

It is thus a *teleological* view of education—learning ordered both toward an overarching moral purpose or goal as well as a spiritual *telos*. (The term *telos* in Greek denotes a "purpose, aim, end, or goal"— terms that I will use interchangeably throughout this book.) For the Platonist, God appears as the final goal of all true learning. All of the liberal arts—and the more specific fields of inquiry—provide pathways by which our minds may travel to God by means of his creation. Liberal education becomes an exercise in ascending from the created world to the uncreated Cause, Source, and Origin of all that is.

St. Augustine of Hippo (354–430 AD) was educated in and taught the classical liberal arts. He was the imperial professor of rhetoric in Milan before his conversion to Christianity. For Augustine, the Platonic view of liberal learning as ascent takes on special significance after his conversion to Christianity and his discovery of Jesus' summary of the "law and the prophets" in the two "greatest" commandments: "To love the Lord your God with all your heart, soul, mind, and strength," and "you shall love your neighbor as yourself" (Matthew 22:34-40). The moral and spiritual purposes of learning find their center in these high and lofty divine commands, and Augustine sets himself to the task of understanding how liberal arts education can lead simultaneously to obedience of these two divine commands and to fulfillment of the deepest teleological moral and spiritual purposes of intellectual beings.

How precisely does a liberal arts education help one to fulfill their ultimate calling to be a good lover of God and neighbor? It does so in two ways, for Augustine. First, learning about the world of nature and culture is an expression of the desire to love both God and neighbor. Careful and patient consideration of God's world in all of its vibrant beauty and bewildering complexity is inherently reverent, worshipful, and honoring of both God and neighbor. By learning about creation, one learns about the Creator. By learning about human culture— and its many expressions throughout history and around the world today—one learns about one's neighbors, and the Creator who created them in his image, calling them to be cocreators with him. Even confused, darkened expressions of human civilization contain rays of truth, goodness, and beauty.

Liberal arts education properly conceived, for Augustine, is not merely learning about the Creator, but, indeed, it is a learning *toward* God and neighbor. Learning consists in both intellectual capacity for knowing but also the will's capacity for loving. Intellect and will (along with memory) are the preeminent powers of the human soul—they must be united for true learning to occur. The attention required to properly understand some feature of the world is thus an expression of desire—desire to understand, desire for God. Genuine learning unites proper knowing with proper loving. The soul possesses the inherent capacity to ascend from knowledge of any particular truth or facet of the world to love for he who is the Source of all that is. One can follow the traces of truth, goodness, and beauty scattered throughout nature and human culture (e.g., social arrangements, art, government, institutions, architecture, literature) to the Source itself. It is a lesson Augustine learned from Plato. By properly tracing these values to their Source in God, one is strengthened in the ability to discern and appreciate the relative value of these earthly things. In the same way, one's knowledge of the world of human culture is an expression of loving, careful attention to one's neighbors, living and dead. Even the capacity to form judgments about the relative value of human culture reveals inwardly a connection to God as the Source of all truth, goodness, and beauty. All truth, beauty, and goodness is God's truth, beauty, and goodness. There is nothing of which one can learn that does not derive its ultimate existence from God.

Thus the second great phase in the soul of education is Augustine's Christian baptism of the liberal arts and reinterpretation of their Platonic moral and spiritual purposes through the lens of the double commandments of love—a reinterpretation of the classical view of the human person that I will explore more fully in the next chapter. The Augustinian Christian vision held sway for over a millennium after Augustine's death in 430 AD, giving rise to the university in the late Middle Ages and to the birth of the Protestant liberal arts college in early modern America.

Modernity witnessed the secularization of the liberal arts—that is, the repudiation of its historical purpose—and the slow erosion of the Augustinian Christian vision of the soul of education. The changing conception of the human person in the wake of scientific naturalism, Enlightenment rationalism, and Romantic individualism tells the story of Augustine's Christian view of liberal learning undergoing full secularization, whereupon love for God and neighbor were replaced by moral autonomy and spiritual authenticity as beacons in the pursuit of knowledge. The Romantic movement in the nineteenth century, especially in thinkers such as Ralph Waldo Emerson, was an inspired attempt to renew the moral and spiritual purposes of liberal arts education and elevate the aim of intellectual life in a time of tremendous economic upheaval in the United States. Emerson's transcendent individual soul and moral authenticity is deeply indebted to the Platonic and Augustinian visions of the moral and spiritual purposes of liberal learning. Emerson offers a metaphysical picture of the individual, shorn of its dogmatic and sectarian Christian commitments, suited to an increasingly pluralistic and secular democratic age. Yet the erosion even of this secularized Augustinian vision over the past one hundred and fifty years suggests that this nonsectarian picture of the moral and spiritual purposes of learning is still too narrow. Liberal arts education today is entrenched in a kind of naturalist secular*ism* that presumes freedom from and neutrality in regard to all spiritual, religious, and metaphysical beliefs, and a kind of materialism with regard to the purposes of human life that has no room for shared or public appeals to transcendence, sacredness, or religious value.

Where is the transcendent or theological framework robust enough to replace the Platonic, Augustinian, or Emersonian visions of the moral and spiritual purposes of a liberal arts education? Losing all sense for the teleology of education threatens to reduce it to an instrumentalized materialist race in which students compete for degrees that entitle them to smart, beautiful lives with respectable careers and paychecks.

Renewing the Augustinian Christian vision

If history is our guide, then we should know this is a crisis of epic proportion—not only for higher education, but for civilization. This is a time of tremendous change in higher education in terms of its intellectual and economic purposes. This is a moment of unprecedented advances at the frontiers of scientific knowledge and economic production. The forces of cultural pluralism, economic globalization, and information technology demand reconsideration of the economic and intellectual questions of education—What should I know? What should I make?—in entirely new ways. How can the connections between these questions and the moral and spiritual purposes of learning be renewed in order to reunite the fourfold purpose of education once more? Much is at stake, including the formation of the next generation in the moral ideals and spiritual values that have formed the social fabric and animated modern democratic life. My argument in this book is that, in order to construct a new connection between the four purposes of learning, there is a readily available therapy in the best of the liberal arts tradition. The life and thought of St. Augustine provides guideposts in the pursuit to renew the conversation and commitment to the fourfold purpose of learning.

Why Augustine?

A similar retrieval could employ other classical authors—such as Plato—or modern authors—such as Emerson—but there are compelling reasons to turn to Augustine as the patron saint of the soul of education today. Paradoxically, Augustine saved liberal arts education from perishing at the end of the Roman Empire by abandoning it. Although I do not want to overdraw the comparison between Augustine's age and the present, there are striking similarities between his narration of liberal arts education at the end of the Roman Empire and this historical moment. In Augustine's telling, the liberal arts had become a hollow shell, detached from their roots in his own lifetime. This drove him to imbue them with new moral and spiritual purpose, refreshing their vitality. He did all of this *after* he quit as imperial professor of rhetoric (rhetoric is the crowning liberal art of eloquence) and began pursuing a Christian version of the liberal arts outside the institutional borders of imperial education.

Because Augustine is perhaps the most famous convert in Christian history, it is easy to miss that his spiritual autobiography, the *Confessions*, is both about his conversion and his lamentation of the lost moral and spiritual purposes of education. His renunciation of a profound academic career should be read, at least in part, as a protest against the moral enervation and vacuity of liberal arts education in the later Roman Empire. Conversion led Augustine to reinvent the moral and spiritual purposes of education and establish the first-ever Christian liberal arts curriculum. Although Augustine ostensibly abandoned this curricular project after his ordination as a priest, one finds throughout his vast corpus of writings a vision of moral and spiritual formation suited to liberal education—a project that never left him even though the context of his classroom changed dramatically as bishop of Hippo. Augustine's educational journey is the story of his restless pursuit of the moral and spiritual purposes of learning.

Augustine's *Confessions*

Augustine was born in the year 354 in the town of Thagaste in what is now Algeria. He lived in the waning years of the Roman Empire and experienced firsthand the tension between pagan and Christian Rome. Born to a Christian mother, Monica, and a pagan father, Patricius, he spent the first three decades of his life running from his mother's faith and chasing ambition, pleasure, and spiritual enlightenment. At the ripe young age of thirty-one he found himself as imperial professor of rhetoric in the capital city of Milan (something akin to being the endowed chair of government at Harvard) and yet somehow felt empty and unfulfilled amidst this massive achievement. He converted to Christianity and moved first to the lake district town of Cassiciacum in Italy and then back to North Africa to pursue liberal arts education in the light of his newfound faith in a community of fellow learners. Eventually, he was ordained—somewhat against his will—as pastor and then bishop of Hippo and spent the rest of his life there in ministry.

Amidst his extensive duties as bishop, Augustine wrote—tirelessly. More of his writings survive, by far, than anyone else in the ancient world: more than 100 treatises, 250 letters, and 1,000 sermons—more than 5 million words in all. After Jesus and Paul, no one has done more than Augustine to shape Western Christianity. Born from real debates in the church, Augustine pioneered the great debates about faith and reason, grace and works, and church and state. And his *Confessions* stands tall among the many works that exert this influence. Although today the genre of spiritual autobiography and spiritual memoir is quite common, the *Confessions* is the very first work of this kind in Western history, an innovation and achievement of form and content that may never be matched.

Given the bright lights of Augustine's conversion scene in book eight of the *Confessions*—where he hears the voice of a child singing "take up and read"—it is easy to lose sight of the book's subplot: the story of the miseducation of a Roman elite. It is the lamentation of one of Rome's "excellent sheep," to borrow William Deresiewicz's contemporary characterization of super-achieving Ivy Leaguers.[2] Augustine's sense of intellectual purpose remains stunted throughout his education due to disconnection from his moral and spiritual aspirations. His intellectual formation was oriented solely toward the external goal of career—the *economic* purpose in the broad sense of money, class, and power and their inseparability in Roman culture. Augustine reports being frustrated by this instrumentalization as a student, yet he so internalizes it, that by the time he is a teacher, he instills it in his own students.

From his first day in school, Augustine laments the disconnection between moral formation and intellectual training. The only kind of

2　William Deresiewicz, *Excellent Sheep: The Miseducation of the American Elite and the Way to a Meaningful Life* (New York: Free Press, 2014).

moral formation he detects at school is obedience training. He learns to obey authority:

> The program for right living presented to me as a boy was that I must obey my mentors, so that I might get on in this world and excel in the skills of the tongue, skills which lead to high repute and deceitful riches. To this end I was sent to school to learn my letters, though I, poor wretch, could see no point in them. (*CF* 1.14)

Augustine particularly bemoans the rough treatment he and his classmates received as punishment for their lazy behavior. Punishment for playing around at school instead of studying struck Augustine as perverse once he began to recognize the higher forms of play among his teachers. Their power to punish was arbitrary and their punishment was hypocritical.

> All the same, we were blameworthy, because we were less assiduous in reading, writing and concentrating on our studies than was expected of us. It was not that we lacked intelligence or ability, Lord, for you had endowed us with these in a measure appropriate to our age; it was simply that we loved to play, and we were punished by adults who nonetheless did the same themselves. But whereas the frivolous pursuits of grown-up people are called "business," children are punished for behaving in the same fashion, and no one is sorry for either the children or the adults; so are we to assume that any sound judge of the matter would think it right for me to be beaten because I played ball as a boy, and was hindered by my game from more rapid progress in studies which would only equip me to play an uglier game? Moreover, was the master who flogged me any better himself? If he had been worsted by a fellow-scholar in some pedantic dispute, would he not have been racked by even more bitter jealousy than I was when my opponent in a game of ball got the better of me? (*CF* 1.15)

Augustine's lamentation strikes the central point. The intellectual purpose of learning has been so thoroughly geared to the economic—

"high repute and deceitful riches"—and so hollowed of a genuine "program for right living" that he could only see it as a falsely dignified and overstuffed game. Education had become a contest of intelligence aimed at a larger cultural charade, a mental competition for the external rewards of prestige, power, and paycheck. Although the aims of his intellectual formation were misdirected, Augustine was grateful nevertheless for the core skills of speaking, writing, and reading he acquired in this period—gifts that he later put to good use (*CF* 1.24).

From an early age, it was clear to himself and his family that Augustine was peculiarly intelligent and gifted with words. Augustine reports that although he hated school, he carried on in academic excellence out of a "vain urge to excel" (*CF* 1.30). The brightest career prospects for such talent in eloquence lay in the field of public affairs— where there was a premium on the ability to persuade an audience.

Augustine came from a middle-class family of modest means, and a good liberal arts education in those days required one to leave home. So Augustine left home for the regional city of Madaura and later the larger metropolis of Carthage. During his spell in Madaura— as a sixteen-year-old—his studies were interrupted by a return trip home: "The reason for this was that my father was saving up to send me farther afield, to Carthage, though it was his shameless ambition that suggested the plan, not his wealth, for he was no more than a fairly obscure town councilor at Thagaste" (*CF* 2.5). Augustine regrets that his father's "only concern was that I should learn to excel in rhetoric and persuasive speech" (*CF* 2.4). Yet Augustine seems to have internalized the purely instrumental view of education propounded by his teachers and father and was fully converted to this vision of education by the time he finished his studies in Carthage:

> The prestigious course of studies I was following looked as its goal to the law-courts, in which I was destined to excel and where I would earn a reputation all the higher in the measure that my

performance was the more unscrupulous. So blind can people be that they glory in their blindness! Already I was the ablest student in the school of rhetoric. At this I was elated and vain and swollen with pride. (*CF* 3.6)

Augustine's mother and father reveal the two purposes to which intellectual formation can be directed: acquisition of economic ends on the one hand, and moral and spiritual development on the other. His father Patricius held an unqualified instrumentalist view of liberal arts education as the pursuit of economic ends, and one can almost feel Augustine's anger in remembering the pressure this exerted.

Both my parents were very keen on my making progress in study: my father, because he thought next to nothing about you and only vain things about me; and my mother, because she regarded the customary course of [liberal] studies as no hindrance, and even a considerable help, toward my gaining you eventually. (*CF* 2.8)

Augustine's mother Monica, however, expected liberal arts education to aim higher, toward the spiritual purpose of "gaining" God himself.

The hollowness of his liberal arts education led Augustine to join an esoteric religious sect called Manicheanism, a cult that viewed the cosmos as a duality of warring oppositions—light and dark, good and evil, material and immaterial—with special focus on spiritual purification through denial of the body. But when Augustine finally met one of the intellectual exemplars of the sect—a Manichean bishop named Faustus—he became sorely disappointed. Faustus was touted as "extremely well informed" in all "branches of reputable scholarship" and particularly "learned in the liberal arts" (*CF* 5.3). But,

[w]hat I found was a man ill-educated in the liberal arts, apart from grammar, and even in that schooled only to an average level. He had read a few of Cicero's speeches and one or two books by Seneca, and some volumes fairly well written in Latin for his own sect, and

because in addition to this he was accustomed to preach daily, he had acquired a fair command of language, which was rendered the more glib and seductive by his skillful management of what ability he had and a certain natural charm. (*CF* 5.11)

By the time of this encounter, Augustine had acquired the skills and commitments needed to see through Faustus, along with the astrological and superstitious pseudo-philosophical myths of the Manichees. His liberal arts education equipped him with skills necessary to pursue truth and metaphysical reality, even as those things related to religion and ultimate matters (*CF* 5.12).

At Carthage, in the advanced course of Augustine's studies in rhetoric—the equivalent of undergraduate study—he discovered Cicero's *Hortensius*. A Platonic exhortation to the philosophical life, the book awakened in Augustine a strong desire for true wisdom—a wisdom behind and beyond mere persuasion—and inspiration to study philosophy. So instead of moving to Italy to pursue a career as a law-court orator, Augustine returned home to Thagaste in Africa to teach the trivium (grammar, logic, and rhetoric) to introductory students. Augustine then moved to Carthage to found his own school of rhetoric for advanced students. He continued there as a teacher for eight years but was disheartened by the rowdiness and ill-preparedness of his students. When the opportunity came to teach rhetoric in Rome, Augustine claimed it. Rome's students were better, he reports in the *Confessions*, but they liked to cheat and often avoided paying tuition. Eventually Symmachus, the mayor of Rome, approached Augustine and offered him a major post in Milan as imperial professor of rhetoric—a much bigger job and great assurance of upward mobility in terms of prestige and pay. But in 384 AD, while in Milan, Augustine's disillusionment with academic careerism hit a fever pitch, so he took up the study of the Platonists (especially the Neoplatonism of Plotinus and Porphyry) in earnest.

What Augustine learns from the Platonists

Augustine's discovery of Platonist philosophy amounted to an intellectual and spiritual breakthrough—especially in terms of how he understood liberal arts education. The moral and spiritual purposes of learning he so longed for finally rose to the surface. The happy life—*beatitudo* or *felicitas* in the Latin of Augustine's translated editions of the Greeks—is a deep and true form of human flourishing that ensues from a life well-lived, a life of moral and intellectual excellence. In his treatise *On Order*—which contains the proposal for a Christian adaptation of the Platonic vision of liberal arts education he drafted in Milan immediately following his conversion—Augustine writes: "[i]nstruction in the liberal arts, in moderation and to the point, produces lively, persevering, and refined lovers of truth. Their aim is ardently to desire, constantly to pursue, and eventually lovingly cling to what is called the happy life" (*OD* 1.24).

For the Platonists, the moral and spiritual purposes of a liberal arts education ultimately converge in *contemplation*—that is, in an unadulterated understanding, awareness, and appreciation of inherent cosmic *order* for its own sake, as its own kind of delight. In essence, the liberal arts have the power to lead the mind to God. A disciplined study of the world should result in a disciplined grasp of reality. Such discipline involves an inward ordering of the soul in greater attunement to the world and greater attunement to the divine order that undergirds it all. Augustine fully adopts this view of the doubled moral *and* spiritual purpose of contemplation and endorses it with his own Christian vision:

> The truly learned are those who, not allowing all the different realities to distract them, attempt their unification into a simple, true, and certain whole. Having done so, they can soar on to divine realities not rashly and by faith alone, but contemplating,

understanding, and retaining them. These realities are forbidden to the slaves of pleasure, or to those hankering after perishing things … To go further, one has to have a good mind, be of mature age, enjoy leisure, and have enthusiasm for study, enough to pursue the order of the disciplines … Getting acquainted with the liberal arts, however, whether pursued for the sake of usefulness or for the sake of knowledge and contemplation, is extremely difficult. It is necessary to be most clever and to start from childhood with unfaltering attention and perseverance. (*OD* 2.44)

It is noteworthy that, in this passage, Augustine views sound intellectual formation through the liberal arts as ordered to both instrumental usefulness and contemplation. The moral-spiritual purpose of contemplation, however, is higher and stands as the terminus of intellectual striving.

What Augustine most treasured in the Platonic picture of liberal arts education was its sense of wholeness: "The truly learned are those who, not allowing all the different realities to distract them, attempt their unification into a simple, true, and certain whole" (*OD* 2.44). This is a picture of reality in which metaphysics (the study of being), epistemology (the study of how we know), and ethics (the study of right living) all connect and interrelate. Intellectual formation in the range of liberal arts disciplines and their interrelation is integrally linked to both the pursuit of a good life and the ascent toward God. The Platonist picture makes the most sense of liberal education's fourfold purpose, in Augustine's eyes, as an interconnected whole— where healthy pursuit of intellectual growth and material security are reconfigured in the light of the highest moral and spiritual aspirations. In the Platonists' implicit hierarchy of purposes, the economic realm matters but remains unclear until the intellect stretches toward the Highest Good. Augustine inherits this metaphysical picture and slowly begins to revise it in the light of his developing understanding of the Christian faith.

What Augustine does not learn from the Platonists

Augustine inherits the Platonic view of liberal education as a progressive ascent that culminates in contemplation of the divine. Contemplative fulfillment is made possible—and the world intelligible—by a vestige of divine order in the human soul. This harmony between Platonism and Christianity, for Augustine, is rooted in a shared anthropology in which human beings are image bearers of the divine. For Platonists, as for Christians, contemplation makes one more like God; it inculcates godlikeness.

Yet Augustine's experiments in the ascent of Platonic liberal arts education in book seven of his *Confessions* leave him unfulfilled in the pursuit of this culminating intellectual vision. He reports coming very close through disciplined study of reality—he catches a glimpse and can still remember the "fragrance"—but ultimately he is forced back from a stable and lasting knowledge of this divine reality.

> Thus I pursued my inquiry by stages, from material things to the soul that perceives them through the body, And from there to that inner power of the soul to which the body's senses report external impressions ... I proceeded further and came to the power of discursive reason, to which the data of our senses are referred for judgment ... and then my mind attained to *That Which Is*, in the flash of one tremulous glance. Then indeed did I perceive your invisible reality through created things, but to keep my gaze there was beyond my strength. I was forced back through weakness and returned to my familiar surroundings, bearing with me only a loving memory, one that yearns for something of which I had caught the fragrance, but could not yet feast upon. (*CF* 7.23)

Augustine says he is beaten back from contemplation—from the contemplative consummation found in the alignment of internal and external order and intellectual and affective awareness of a divine designer. This holy frustration in learning, this lack of consummation for his active intellect, corroborates the Scriptural truth of Incarnation.

In the Incarnation of Jesus Christ, Augustine believes, the upward movement of intellectual ascent culminates in the downward movement of divine descent—God is revealed as a person who forms the bridge on which the weakened human intellect crosses over to behold the Highest Good face to face.

> There are two ways of getting through this darkness [toward divine contemplation]: either by reasoning or by certain authority. Philosophy does it by reasoning, but brings freedom to very few. It forces these few not only into not despising those mysteries, but to understand them insofar as possible. True and, so to speak, genuine philosophy can do no more than teach the First Principle of all things, itself without principle; what great knowledge is in it, and what riches issue from there for our immense benefit and without decrease on its part! This is none other than the one God almighty and thrice powerful, Father, Son, and Holy Spirit ... And how great, to cap it all, is the mystery of the Incarnation. For our sake God lowered himself to assuming a human body. The more demeaning such a thing appears, the more merciful and the farther away and out of the grasp of proud minds it is. (*OD* 2.16)

From the Platonists, Augustine says, he glimpses the moral-spiritual goal of divine contemplation, but not the way there. By the Incarnation Augustine learns that the high spiritual purpose of liberal arts education is not ultimately found in rational pursuit of the prime knowledge Object but rather in relationship to the ultimate Subject who initiates and acts. The ramifications of Incarnation for education—especially for the moral-spiritual purpose of contemplation—are vast and I will continue to explore them throughout this book, but let me highlight the heart of the matter here.

Although Augustine finds the Platonist's moral-spiritual purpose of contemplation a huge advance over his own instrumental sense of the liberal arts, his experience of being "beaten back" from the goal and his newfound faith reveal a new angle on the virtue of intellectual humility in liberal education. Unlike Socratic skepticism—"I know that I don't know anything"—Augustine's sense of intellectual humility is best understood as a kind of radical awe or wonder in the face of ultimate reality that is experienced as one's place before God. This awareness, coupled with a sense of divine intimacy and approachability in the Incarnation, puts one in the proper intellectual posture to receive contemplative vision as a divine gift.

This experience teaches Augustine both the limits of reason as a mechanism for ascent and highlights the necessity and importance of faith in one's approach toward the moral-spiritual goal. Belief, for Augustine, is the ability to trust in that which has been revealed about the divine (in his case the historical event of the Incarnation: Christ's life, death, and resurrection) and represents a necessary element in one's pursuit of ultimate understanding or divine contemplation. Ascent to a contemplative vision of the divine order in all that is requires both illumination by reason and humble trust in that which can only be taught on the basis of authority (for him, Scripture and Christian doctrine encapsulated in the creeds). Motivated by awed acknowledgment of one's place in a masterful and vast cosmic mystery, ascent requires humble submission to another's teaching on the basis of authority. It is not an unbridled appeal to arbitrary gullibility on Augustine's part, but a sensitive picture of the soul's ascent in learning through reason and trust in authority. In other words, contemplation, or the moral-spiritual purpose of liberal arts education, is best pursued by faith seeking understanding.

Augustine's experience of the limits of contemplative ascent and the truth of Incarnation free him from what he sees as the Platonic fantasy of a harmonious natural liberal arts theology by which the mind moves seamlessly from the visible to the invisible, from the created to the uncreated, toward absolute knowledge of *That Which*

Is—a "knowledge of your invisible reality through created things" (*CF* 7.23). His insistence on humility and faith as constitutive elements in the contemplative fulfillment of learning deflates some of the spiritual ambition and confidence found in the Platonic picture, shrouding it in a new sense of modesty and mystery better suited to the enterprise of liberal arts education and the knowledge of God.

Faith should make room for humble acceptance of the mystery of ultimate reality and appreciative tolerance for competing visions of learning's ultimate fulfillment. Augustine strips the Platonist's moral-spiritual purpose of its rational mysticism—freeing it from the despair that ensues in the discovery that there is no purely rational ascent from knowledge of the disciplines to God's nature. This despair quickly pivots toward the nihilistic belief that because there is no purely rational ascent, there must be no transcendent aim or purpose for education. Augustine's emphasis on the Incarnation of the Word leads to an increasing sensitivity to the ways in which knowledge of the divine—the ultimate goal—always requires faith, and for him, is always encoded in the words of Scripture, enigmatically recording the events that bring one to the core of God's self-revelation. If contemplation of the divine is the Object of learning, the Incarnation brings that Subject to the enfleshed and sensible world in a new way. It is no longer solely the story of humankind's rational search for God, but God's loving search for humankind. As Augustine progresses in his Christian faith, he becomes more suspicious of the Platonic view of a solitary, wordless, disembodied, rational ascent to God and godlikeness. Augustine's Christian faith loosens the tidy Platonic picture and creates more room for the mystery of truth, bodily life, and human happiness in its recognizably earthly forms. I will turn to these refinements of the Platonic picture in the following chapters. Even so, what Augustine gains from the Platonic picture of ultimate learning is vast and essential. It is the interconnectedness of all things and the interrelation of the four purposes of learning.

Augustine's journey in the *Confessions* is transformation from excellent sheep to restless heart. It is the story of not only his own education but his role as an educator in the liberal arts. It is a story that climaxes in his discovery of the Platonists and his conversion to Christianity as well as his conception of a form of Christian liberal arts education outside the matrix of instrumental Roman education—and far outside the conventional institutional channels of imperial liberal education.

What we can learn from Augustine

Turning to Augustine in the present makes sense, given his vast influence not only in the history of Christianity but in the history of education. Shrouded now as it may be, Augustine's vision of liberal arts education is the moral and spiritual background of the contemporary college and university. It was Augustine's innovative Christian adaptation of the Platonist moral and spiritual purposes of learning that gave birth to the medieval university and Protestant liberal arts college in early modern America—a vision that has been slowly secularized and eroded over the past 200 years. Augustine's life and thought reveals that liberal arts education is inherently moral and spiritual—that is, to do liberal arts education presupposes answers to the questions of learning's moral and spiritual purposes. To deny this or to pretend that it is otherwise is to do something other than liberal arts education. Answers are always being offered—no matter what— and if left unacknowledged as a core element of the project of liberal learning, they will remain mere semblances of what they should be.

This is the crisis facing higher education, that the instrumentalization of education presumes an implicit, inarticulate, unexamined answer to the questions: What should I do? Who or what should I worship? Augustine's testimony from 1600 years ago suggests that this crisis is nothing new. Losing the purpose of learning is a perennial challenge. Proceeding as if liberal arts education is not inherently and irreducibly connected to the moral and spiritual is to convert it into something more akin to trade school—a place where students are making things but not being made into anything. There is nothing wrong with trade school, but such training could be completed much more cheaply if it were stripped of the veneer, expensive accoutrements, and cultural prestige. Thus, the call to recover the Augustinian vision of education amounts to a gauntlet thrown to liberal arts institutions to make their own animating visions clearer and propose answers to the questions of learning's moral and spiritual purposes, rather than satisfying themselves with justification for intellectual purpose through the lens of economy. Moral and spiritual questions of purpose are not ancillary to liberal arts education. Many liberal arts colleges and universities—both secular and religious—are trying to keep these questions alive (or the four purposes together), often through the medium of the core curriculum, but such attempts often fall short of becoming a whole or inspiring vision. The challenge is wholeness and inspiration. Augustine's vision offers both.

From Augustine there is a single insight that he borrowed from the Platonists that may be gleaned as an antidote for the present age's great instrumentalization of education: the idea of an inherent connection in all things. Augustine restlessly searches through his studies for one architectonic idea that will bring everything together, that will offer a grand sense of coherence: where there is a connection among subjects, connection among the purposes of learning, and connection between himself and all that can be learned. The ground and glue of creation—in all its diversity and profusion and beauty—is God, the ultimate Subject of inquiry. God stands over and within all other subjects of inquiry. This produces a radical sense of wonder in Augustine—a grounding disposition for his inquiry into all branches of learning. This sense of connection reveals Augustine's place before the ultimate Subject of inquiry, and humble recognition of the divine craftsmanship, causality, and containment of all things grants him a keen sense of his relation not only to God but to all of the other things about which he can learn. This rational and affective appreciation for connection is what makes liberal arts education properly moral, in Augustine's eyes, for it allows one to recognize one's place in and responsibility to the order of things.

Augustine's thoughts about the liberal arts in the *Confessions* echo the Roman philosopher Seneca's lamentation over fragmentated education:

> The question has been posed whether these liberal arts studies make a man a better person. But in fact they do not aspire to any knowledge of how to do this, let alone claim to do this … If you really want to know how far [the teachers of the liberal arts] are from the position of being moral teachers, observe the absence of connection between all the things they study; if they were teaching one and the same thing a connection would be evident. (Seneca, *Letter* 88)

Seneca's Letter 88 drips with cynical criticism of Roman liberal arts education on just this point—there is no connection between liberal arts education and character formation insofar as none of the teachers connect all the subjects of their studies. The camps of academic expertise in the Roman Empire, and in the present day, reveal more than the fragmentation of disciplinary inquiry: They betray an inability to connect education with character formation. I will turn to the question of liberal arts education and character formation in the next chapter.

Antidote for our own age

The sense of connection that can be gleaned from Augustine's journey is the antidote for the present age. Augustine's miseducation allows one to see what a great disservice is done to students when they are offered a purely instrumental description of the value of education, and there is silence about the inherently moral and spiritual purposes of learning. For without any intelligible account of learning's moral and spiritual purposes, the justification for the intellectual purpose of liberal arts education is submerged solely in the instrumental, economic, and external—when we make these moves, we still offer implicit answers to the moral and spiritual questions: What should I do? Who or what should I worship?

America has witnessed a recent spate of thoughtful reflection on the hollowness and pervasiveness of an achievement culture in higher education, and the clever careerist students that know how best to climb the system. These "exemplary" students are the products of this culture's instrumental view of education. William Deresiewicz's *Excellent Sheep* is a stunning view inside the over-achieving lives of this generation's most competitive students—those who make it into the Ivy League. These are students, like Augustine, who are not only over-achievers, they are super-achievers. They have learned three languages, launched a small tech start-up, mastered all of Chopin's piano concertos, and traveled to the North Pole to study arctic fauna even before they apply. These are thinkers and learners who have so thoroughly internalized the instrumentalist picture of higher education as career and achievement preparation that they seemingly do not need the four-year experience of college apart from the instrumental opportunity for elite networking that it affords.

Super students are devoted to the "résumé virtues rather than the eulogy virtues," to use David Brooks's helpful phrase:

> The résumé virtues are the ones you list on your résumé, the skills that you bring to the job market and that contribute to external success. The eulogy virtues are deeper. They're the virtues that get talked about at your funeral, the ones that exist at the core of your being—whether you are kind, brave, honest or faithful; what kinds of relationships you formed.[3]

---

[3]   David Brooks, *The Road to Character* (New York: Random House, 2015), xi.

It makes sense that the best college students are devoted almost single-mindedly to their résumé virtues. They have been given an educational system that provides no other, broader, deeper sense of the purpose of education; no sense of connection; no space to reflect on the moral and spiritual purposes of learning, and they have been promised a degree that will provide them with real value in the form of economic return on investment.

Such an educational system reflects back the most deeply cherished and commonly held values and beliefs about the world in American culture. Such values produce students who are increasingly uninterested in learning for its own sake, submerged in grade calculation, outside career networking, and material achievements. There is nothing wrong with networking and achievement if they are done in service of a higher purpose. Do such students have a higher purpose? The crisis is that the economic purpose, what I call the manufacturing *telos*, has reduced the three other questions of higher education's value—What should I know? What should I do? Who or what should I worship?—to a single, utility-minded concern: What will I make? Even the tense of the question shifts away from moral concern for the present to a future vision of acquisition. As Allan Bloom writes in *The Closing of the American Mind*, "Every education system has a moral goal that it tries to attain. It wants to produce a certain kind of human being. This intention is more or less explicit, more or less a result of reflection; but even the neutral subjects, like reading, writing, and arithmetic, take their place in their vision of the educated person."[4] There is no neutral ground in higher education. Educational institutions are always forming and shaping a certain kind of person, and even without a pursuit of moral knowledge, there is always an implicit moral and spiritual vision that undergirds

---

[4] Allan Bloom, *The Closing of the American Mind: How Higher Education Has Failed Democracy and Impoverished the Souls of Today's Students* (New York: Simon & Schuster, 1987), 26.

the work of learning. Excellent sheep are the kinds of people that a purely instrumentalized understanding of liberal arts education produces.

By presuming to evade the questions of moral and spiritual purpose the purely instrumentalized view of education enshrines economic value as the moral and spiritual purpose of liberal education. By this I do not mean to suggest that there are no educators left who preach the value of learning for its own sake or who embody a vision of the intrinsic value of liberal arts education ordered toward higher goods. Assuredly higher education is full of these sorts of teachers—just consider the meager salaries of many professors. Yet it is surprising how silent and inarticulate many teachers and administrators are when it comes to explaining the moral and spiritual purposes of the enterprise.

Many have become rightly suspicious of the kind of college professor who deconstructs everything and then starts talking about the universal meaning of life—as if a crusty Shakespeare professor with soft hands holds the keys of wisdom. Indeed, in higher education there seems to be a full and final disconnection between learning and morality—between knowledge and wisdom. No one dare ask their professor for spiritual advice. Yet ironically this comes at a time in our culture when secularization has shifted much of the cultural authority for matters of morality and the life of the spirit into the hands of such experts, making college the new temple and professors its priests. Indeed, many professors preach a form of intolerant tolerance toward any ideas outside the mainstream of liberal progressive politics, providing a kind of formation for their students. And students can be very good disciples—take, for example, the recent student protests and demonstrations at Middlebury College against any expression of ideas that do not agree with and support their own progressive values. Such protests amount to deep moral energy closed to further inquiry.

Explicit answers to the questions of the moral and spiritual purposes of liberal learning must be given. Today, liberal arts education seems stuck between an increasingly hollow form of clever careerism (the moral formation provided by a thoroughly instrumentalized view of education) and a sharpened moral progressivism that demands perfection and purity of ideas in society and on campus. Is there a way beyond these to another option? Augustine's journey provides a clue. College ought not be a pen of excellent sheep or a guild of progressive acolytes but rather a restless hearts club—a unique institution devoted to the widest learning possible, unafraid to ask the biggest questions in the most rigorous way.

Colleges are unique institutions historically—often related to the church yet serving a separate mission, a place where questions and inquiry lead the way, a place where the enterprise of learning touches the third rail of morality and spiritual life. The intellectual role of the college is distinct but complements the pastoral role of the church: Each pursues the great end of contemplation but from different starting points, along different paths. Augustine's personal advance beyond the Platonic view of the spiritual purpose of liberal arts education—into the terrain where faith is required—speaks to another antidote that the Augustinian vision of liberal arts education might provide for the present: the importance of faith—of faith seeking understanding—as a framework for thinking about the moral and spiritual purposes of liberal education.

A range of secular authors—for example, David Brooks and Wiliam Deresiewicz—have recently praised faith-based liberal arts colleges as one of the last bastions of holistic formation, places where intellectual inquiry remains yoked to moral formation and spiritual aspiration beyond instrumental concerns. Such unlikely praise is welcome encouragement for Christian liberal arts colleges, but is the praise warranted? The Augustinian vision of liberal arts education—one that requires religious faith as the frame that holds the four questions together—is the way forward as a model for liberal arts education. It certainly presents a challenge to a purely secularist vision of liberal arts education that is either silent about or openly rejects the move to link the economic and intellectual purposes of learning with the moral and spiritual. It is a challenge to take up the conversation and become articulate once more, and to make explicit the moral and spiritual purposes that animate liberal arts education. The Augustinian vision is also a challenge to faith-based liberal arts colleges—especially Christian ones—which pride themselves on the connection of these fourfold purposes in their mission, vision, and values. Do these expressed purposes make a difference in practice? Do they filter down? Do they form the fabric of learning and a coherent way of life?

An Augustinian liberal arts college should be at the vanguard of liberal arts education, demonstrating that learning happens best when there are limits and constraints that make, what Alasdair MacIntyre calls, "constrained" agreement and disagreement possible.[5] Such constraints make substantive moral and spiritual inquiry within the curriculum meaningful, according to MacIntyre. The modern secular university aspires to be a place of unconstrained agreement and has thus abolished all religious and moral statements and exclusions. Yet counterintuitively, MacIntyre argues, this has not led to a deepening of liberal education or agreement about moral and spiritual matters but to a flattening, an endangering of the very enterprise and the humanistic values necessary to sustain it. What is needed, thinkers such as MacIntyre and Brooks argue, are places of shared frameworks and constrained agreements about revisable sets of beliefs and practices that provide the starting point for a common inquiry and debate—in short, new forms of tradition-shaped liberal arts education. The relationship between the kind of religious authority mentioned

5 Alasdair MacIntyre, *Three Rival Versions of Moral Enquiry: Encyclopaedia, Genealogy, and Tradition* (Notre Dame, IN: University of Notre Dame Press, 1990), 230-1.

above and the ongoing revisability of beliefs is the central tension that animates an Augustinian liberal education. Humility renders all knowledge provisional in the faith-filled sense, for Augustine, and faith names not an arrogance of certainty but a tireless starting point in pursuit of deeper understanding.

The Augustinian Christian vision is one option among such tradition-shaped approaches that might be selected to animate the enterprise of liberal education once more. My argument in the remainder of this book is that it should be seriously considered, for it coherently connects the four purposes of learning and it has had tremendous influence in the history of Western liberal arts education—its vital seeds of influence lay dormant and are ready to give life once more.

2

Education and the Order of Love

It seems to me that a brief and true definition of virtue is "rightly ordered love."

Augustine, CG 15.22

Because we cannot at present see what is to be taught, let our part and duty be in desire. The whole life of a good Christian is holy desire. What you at present long for, you do not yet see: by longing, though, you are made capable: so that when that has come which you may see, you can be filled. For just as, if you would fill a bag, and also know how great the thing is to fill it, you stretch the opening of the sack or the skin, or whatever else it be, to make it capable of holding more: so God, by deferring our hope, stretches our desire. And by that desiring, actually stretches the mind. And by that stretching, actually make it more capacious.

Augustine, HFJ 4.6

Introduction

After exploring the contemporary crisis in higher education we see that the challenge to justify the value of a college education is not unique to the present time but, in fact, an abiding, perennial concern. At the heart of it is the question of how to define the intrinsic moral and spiritual values of education and orient the intellectual and economic ends of education toward learning's deeper purposes.

The most profound and lasting picture of the moral and spiritual purposes of liberal arts education in the Western tradition is the Augustinian Christian vision—the one that forms the foundation of the university and liberal arts college in Europe and America. In that vision, intellectual inquiry is ordered toward the moral and spiritual goals of a happy life (*beatitudo* or *felicitas* in Augustine's Latin) and contemplation of the divine order, interpreted through the double commandments of love: "You shall love the Lord your God with all your heart, and with all your soul, and with all your mind ... and You shall love your neighbor as yourself" (Matthew 22:37-39).

If Chapter 1 is a structural and schematic look at those perennially lost purposes of learning—and Augustine's personal struggle to arrive at a view that integrates the four purposes—this chapter is a look at the same journey from *within* the soul, in the contours of the heart, through the lens of Augustine's theory of properly ordered love. What does properly ordered love in the context of liberal education consist in? How does study in the liberal arts help shape and order one's loves?

Ordered love within the context of liberal arts education moves in three directions. First is the inward ordering of the soul that happens as one acquires the moral and intellectual virtues necessary for disciplined study. Second is the upward ordering of love for God—a fulfillment of the command to love God with one's whole mind. Third is the outward ordering of affection for other human beings and one's sense of ethical responsibility to use education in service of the neighbor. This chapter is a meditation on properly ordered love of learning that leads more fully to love for God, neighbor, and healthy self-love.

Inwardly ordered love and liberal arts education

A liberal arts education is a "temporal good," in Augustine's eyes, akin to other temporal goods such as a healthy body, political liberty, and a sufficient supply of friends and wealth. Goods of this kind are "neutral" in the sense that they can be put to either good or bad use. They are inextinguishably good insofar as they are part of God's good created world, yet their situational goodness depends on the character of their user. The great challenge and essential task of a moral and spiritual life, Augustine believes, is learning how to properly use such goods. Virtuous use begins with learning to recognize the value of temporal goods in relation to each other and discerning how to put them toward their intended use. Augustine provides an overview of this process in his treatise *On Christian Teaching*.

> Living a just and holy life requires one to be capable of an objective and impartial evaluation of things; to love things, that is to say, in the right order, so that you do not love what is not to be loved, or fail to love what is to be loved, or have a greater love for what should be loved less, or an equal love for things that should be loved less or more, or a lesser or greater love for things that should be loved equally. (*CT* 1.26-27)

Well-formed love entails both intellectual and affective movements: first, an impartial evaluation of things within the hierarchy of being, and, second, a corresponding alignment of one's affection in accord with the relative merit of the thing itself.

Inward ordering of mind and affections

Liberal arts education is not only a temporal good of its own but also a process through which one learns to recognize the hierarchical order of value in the world. It requires that one orders one's mind and affections so that she can recognize the order of reality or, what Augustine calls, the truth about the world. Not to be confused with a once-and-for-all, totalized conceptual scheme, the mental and affective ordering required for liberal education turns on attention to the world's wholeness of meaning rather than its separate pieces.

Ordering the mind requires *asceticism*: a routine or pattern of life with practices, habits, and virtues that positions one to be receptive to truth. The seven liberal arts—the trivium (the study of language's relationship to reality) and the quadrivium (the study of the measure of quantity) and the many subareas of specialized inquiry that emerge from these seven—are "disciplines." The Latin term *disciplina* from which the English word "discipline" comes means both a branch of knowledge as well as the ordered way of life required for pursuing that kind of knowledge. Achieving discipline in one's life—by successfully marshaling the requirements of leisure and space and moderation of appetites as a participant in a community of fellow learners—generally precedes the intellectual discipline that allows the various branches of learning to find their common root in the mind.

Augustine thinks this requires total commitment to a way of life: "priority must be given to acquiring good habits ... [and we must] resolve not to prefer anything to the search for truth, nor to desire, to think about, or love anything else" (*OD* 2.52). Searching for truth has as much to do with appetite as it does with intelligence. Shortly after his conversion in Milan and retirement from his imperial academic career, Augustine moved to the lake district in Northern Italy to found an experimental community devoted to devising and practicing a Christian liberal arts curriculum—something that did not exist in Augustine's day. In his treatise called *On Order,* he lays out the task to those who would take up this liberal arts education and the discipline it would require to follow in a thoroughly Christian spirit. He calls this the "double order" of liberal arts discipline in "life and learning."

> Discipline ... [is] transcribed in wise souls. They will know how to live and at what high level, in direct proportion to how perfectly they contemplate it and how diligently they keep it in their lives. To those who wish to know it, this discipline imposes a double order: of life and learning. You, its youthful students, must begin

by abstaining from sex, from the enticement of gluttony and drunkenness, the immodest and undue care of body and dress, vain sports and games, the torpor of excess sleep and laziness, ill-natured rivalry, detraction, envy, ambition for office and power, down to excessive desire for simple praise. Know that the love of money is the certain ruin of all your hopes ... Ignore the proud, and above all do not be proud yourself. Live in an orderly and harmonious way. Worship, think about and love God with the support of faith, hope, and love. Pursue peace and due order in your studies, those of your friends and whoever else has talent, with a view to a good mind and a quiet life. (*OD* 2.25)

Augustine's view of the double order of discipline in life and learning required for genuine liberal arts education presupposes a commitment to the metaphysical existence of truth as the discovery of a divinely ordered reality. Knowledge of truth is the intelligible representation of that order within the human soul, made expressible through language. Without these premises, his interconnected picture of loving and learning falls apart.

Internal shaping makes one more susceptible to external reality in its fullness—in itself, for its own sake—rather than as an object to be used for one's private purposes. Refining one's love of truth is both an intellectual and moral act, for Augustine.

The truly learned are those who, not allowing all the different realities to distract them, attempt their unification into a simple, true, and certain whole. Having done so, they can soar on to divine realities not rashly and by faith alone, but contemplating, understanding, and retaining them. These realities are forbidden to the slaves of pleasure, or to those hankering after perishing things ... To go further, one has to have a good mind, be of mature age, enjoy leisure, and have enthusiasm for study, enough to pursue *the order of the disciplines* ... Getting acquainted with the liberal arts, however, whether pursued for the sake of *usefulness* or for the sake of knowledge and *contemplation*, is extremely difficult. It is necessary to be most clever and to start from childhood with unfaltering *attention* and *perseverance*. (*OD* 2.44; my emphasis)

The kinds of habits and excellences required to make progress in study—for example, attention, perseverance, ability to delay gratification, patience—shape one's affections and order one's loves.

One's love of truth manifests in a love of learning, according to Augustine. Love of learning is a hallmark of human nature as a whole and is one of its distinctive features, one by which humans resemble the divine. "All human beings by nature desire to know," Aristotle claims in his *Metaphysics*. Augustine agrees wholeheartedly with him and thinks that deepest human fulfillment and satisfaction come through sharpened capacity to learn.

Studious people exhibit a special sort of love (*amor studentium*)—the peculiar desire found in those who know just enough to know what they do not yet know and what they want to learn. Augustine calls them "people who do not yet know but still desire to know some branch of learning" (*T* 10.1). Yet how can one love something if they do not already know or understand it? Augustine thinks this is the paradox of the desire to learn, akin to the desire for God. Love for God moves by partial and incomplete knowledge, just as one must patiently pursue branches of learning while being an amateur in the discipline.

As for branches of learning, our interest in studying them is very often aroused by the authority of those who commend and popularize them; and yet unless we had at least some slight notion of any subject impressed on our consciousness, it would be quite impossible for us to be kindled with enthusiasm for studying it. Would anyone take any trouble or care to learn rhetoric, for example, unless he knew beforehand that it was the science of speaking? Sometimes too we are amazed at what we hear or experience about the results of these disciplines, and this makes us enthusiastic to acquire by study the means of being able to reach such results ourselves. Suppose someone who does not know about writing is told that it is a discipline by which you can make words in silence with your hand and send them to somebody else a long way away, and by which this person they are sent to can pick them up not with his ears but his eyes; surely when he longs to know how he can do that himself, his enthusiasm is stirred by that result which he has now got the message about. This is the kind of way the enthusiasm and studiousness of learners is enkindled. What you are absolutely ignorant of you simply cannot love in any sense whatever. (*T* 10.1)

Augustine's view of love for study does not presuppose the Platonic doctrine of recollection, but rather is rooted in a view of the human person as *made in the image of God* (Genesis 1:26-27). Divine resemblance manifests in a predisposition to love study and to love God and is rooted in the imprint of divine intelligence on the human soul. The human soul is tripartite, according to Augustine—a triad of intellect, will, and memory. In knowing the three faculties in the soul work in concert.

Human resemblance of the Trinitarian image, however, is not found in the tripartite nature of the soul, for Augustine, but rather is glimpsed in the inner trinity formed by the learning mind. Whenever one learns about reality, there are three inseparable components: mind itself, the mind's knowledge, and self-love (*mens, notitia sui, amor sui*) (*T* 9.1).

In the act of learning, the soul uses its intellect to make a judgment about truth, and uses the will to make an affective judgment about value. Knowledge, Augustine says, consists in a mental word (*verbum mentis*) or image of the thing known in the light of eternal truth, and this word becomes "loved knowledge" (*amata notitia*) insofar as one recognizes it as one's own knowledge. Thus, in every act of knowing one finds an inner trinity: mind's knowledge, the inner word spoken by reason, and the mind's own love for the mental image within (*T* 9.2).

This inner trinity and the knowledge formed in the light of eternal truth highlight why inward ordering of mind and affection is so central to Augustine's vision of education. The capacity to know the world is integrally bound up with one's sense of self-love and one's capacity to recognize and love the praiseworthy. The soul is designed to be unified in the pursuit of the true and the good. The inseparability of the mind's affective and intellectual movements reveals the intimate bond of selfhood, for Augustine, akin to the relationship between the three persons of the Trinity.

Disordered love of learning

Although Augustine presents himself as very clever and career-minded in his pursuit of a liberal arts education, he bemoans how out of sync his intellectual and moral developments became over the course of his studies—reaching their crescendo in his college days at Carthage, where he boiled in the cauldron of disordered desire.

> So I arrived at Carthage, where the din of scandalous love affairs raged cauldron-like around me. I was not yet in love, but I was enamored with the idea of love, and so deep within me was my need that I hated myself for the sluggishness of my desires. In love with loving, I was casting about for something to love … yet this inner famine created no pangs of hunger in me. I had no desire for the food that does not perish, not because I had my fill of it, but because the more empty I was, the more I turned from it in revulsion. My soul's health was consequently poor. It was covered with sores and flung itself out of doors, longing to soothe its misery by rubbing against sensible things; yet these were soulless, and so could not truly be loved. (*CF* 3.1)

Augustine presents his inner turmoil at the outset of book three in *Confessions* in order to highlight the inherent disconnection between the intellectual elements of his liberal arts education and his character formation. He makes progress and has success in terms of intellectual achievement and career prospects, but his interior life starves. Where is the inward ordering of both mind and affections that genuine education promises? He did not find it at Carthage. In Augustine's frenzied depiction of carnal desire and his inability to direct even this carnal passion, one senses the acute impotence of will and disjunction between reason and affection.

This disjunction is evidence of a wounded human nature, in Augustine's account: One can become very clever in terms of intellectual knowledge and technical mastery of the world yet lack knowledge and mastery of their corresponding moral and spiritual purposes. Temptations lurk on every side in liberal arts education: One might pursue knowledge for its own sake as a kind of vain curiosity that preoccupies attention away from the more pressing matters of love and responsibility; one might pursue intellectual and technical mastery of the world as a kind of prideful domination; or one might purse knowledge solely for the instrumental benefits of salary as a form of greed or for prestige and cultural authority in prideful self-assertion.

Augustine's *Confessions* drip with moral realism about the many modes and motives for liberal arts education and how peculiarly difficult it is to properly orient love of learning toward love for God and neighbor. He offers his famous prayer of delay—"Grant me chastity and self-control, Lord, but please not yet" (*CF* 8.17)—for those who want to clean up after four years of freedom. He offers the prayer also as a lament for his own intellectual misadventure during which he acquired an incredible set of material accomplishments and intellectual achievements without making progress on the internal and eternal journey of ordered love.

If things are ultimately unified at the highest level of being, how is it that intellectual mastery of the world and career achievement can proceed without necessary and corresponding advances in ordered affection—the work of properly ordered love? What does properly ordered love for the goods of liberal education look like? This is the question that haunted Augustine's intellectual formation and becomes the central question about education in his *Confessions*. He sets himself the task of answering this question in concrete terms just after his conversion, in his earliest writings, where he attempts a Christian liberal arts curriculum at Cassiciacum and then Thagaste. In these two communities, Augustine gathered with his closest friends and their families and engaged in a common life of learning and daily discipline—as well as the common habits of meals and visits to the bathhouse—aimed at the common goal of ordered love.

The bridge between liberal education and character formation, he discovered, is found in obedience to the twin commandments of love for God and neighbor. Getting the inward movement of liberal education—the inward ordering of mind and affection—is only possible as one moves upward and outward. The virtue of properly ordered love in the context of liberal arts education is a properly formed love of learning that leads more fully to love for God, neighbor, and thereby to a healthy form of self-love. Thus, the journey of properly formed love of learning that leads to love for God, self, and neighbor is not so much a matter of properly ordered love but rather reordered love for liberal arts education illuminated by the twin commandments.

Upward ordering: Liberal education and the love of God

Underneath Augustine's project in *On Order* is the simple conviction that if properly enacted—in life and learning—a thoroughly wide and rigorous course of liberal studies will allow one to "proceed from corporeal to incorporeal realities" (*R* 1.3). As noted above,

Augustine weaves together a biblical understanding of God with a Platonic sense of the divine as the Highest Good from whom all cosmic order and desirable goods on earth derive their goodness and intelligibility.

> There is a Good of all good, from which all good derives, the Good to which nothing can be added to explain what goodness is. For a person is described as good, and a field as good, and a house as good, and an animal as good, and a tree as good, and a body as good, and a soul as good; and every time you said "good," you added something. But there is a simple good, sheer Goodness-Itself, in virtue of which all things are good, the Good itself from which all good things derive their goodness. (*EP* 26(2).8)

The good of learning which is made possible by the good of intellect and the goodness of cosmic order must be directed to God by grateful awareness that even the capacity to learn is a gift. Without a keystone love for God as the highest good, one undermines his ability to make evaluative distinctions about the relative merit of other goods.

> Whatever God has made is good. Some are great goods, some are small goods, but all are good. Some are celestial good things, some are earthly good things; some are spiritual goods, some are bodily goods; some are eternal goods, some are temporal goods. But they are all good, because the one who is good made them good. And so it says somewhere in the divine scriptures, *Set love in order toward me* (Song of Songs 2:4). God made you as something good under him, and he made something lower on the scale, under you as well. You are under one, you are over another. Don't give up the higher good and bow yourself down to the lower good. Be upright, and so be praised, because *all the upright of heart shall be praised* (Ps 64:10). How is it that you sin, after all, but by treating the things you have received for your use in a disordered way, or out of turn? Be a good user of lower things, and you will be an upright enjoyer of the higher good. (*S* 21.3)

Without one's greatest affection fixed on the highest good, in Augustine's view, one's moral life is prone to fragmentation and chaos.

Contemplation and ascent

All of the liberal disciplines provide pathways by which the mind may travel to God by means of his creation—opportunities to "proceed from corporeal to incorporeal realities" as one becomes more and more a "refined lover of truth." The mind has an inherent capacity to ascend from knowledge of any particular truth or facet of the world by love toward he who is the Source.

> It is a thing great and most rare for a man, after he has contemplated the whole corporeal and incorporeal creation and found it mutable, to pass beyond it by effort of mind and arrive at the immutable substance of God, there to learn from God Himself that every nature which is not what God is has been made by Him alone ... [For] He speaks by truth itself, if anyone is able to hear Him with the mind rather than with the body: He speaks to that in man which is better than every other part of him which makes him a man, and than which there is nothing better save God alone. For since man is most rightly understood—or, if that cannot be, then at least believed—to be made in the image of God, there is no doubt that he is brought closer to God by that part of him whereby he rises above the lower parts which he has in common with the beasts ... Of all visible things, the world is the greatest; of all invisible things, the greatest is God ... For, even leaving aside the voices of the [Scriptures], the world itself, by the perfect order of its changes and motions, and by the great beauty of all things visible, proclaims by a kind of silent testimony of its own both that it has been created, and also that it could not have been made other than by a God ineffable and invisible in greatness, and ineffable and invisible in beauty. (*CG* 11.2,4)

One follows traces of truth, goodness, and beauty toward their Source through knowledge—that is, by the capacity to make evaluative judgments about truth and to form bonds of affection in a world replete with varying values. There is nothing of which one can learn that does not ultimately trace its being to God.

Here one glimpses again the spiritual purpose of learning in full illumination, and the fourth question of true education: Who or what should I worship? "Worship, think about and love God," Augustine writes to the "youthful students" of the liberal arts in his treatise *On Order* (2.25). Worship of God is, in Augustine's eyes, the culmination of affection and reason—where the soul finds rest in the ultimate Source of truth and value. Augustine's opening line in *Confessions* is a quotation from the Psalms: "Great are you, O Lord, and exceedingly worthy of praise." Taken together with the final line of that same first paragraph, the two utterances present the *telos* of intellectual inquiry in praise and rest: "our heart is unquiet until it rests in you" (*CF* 1.1). Humans were made to praise, and one's deepest soul satisfaction comes in the contemporaneous dynamic of restless and restful intellectual worship, a kind of worship that results from having one's mind attuned and sharpened to recognize God in the world—in one's self, in Scripture, and in the natural order.

Human beings, Augustine believed, are designed to make evaluative judgments about the world (good and evil, true and false, beautiful and ugly, etc.) and are inclined to revere that which they find praiseworthy. We are evaluative lovers who give time, energy, and attention to the things we find most praiseworthy. Given the limitations of both time and resources—and the nature of human finitude—a liberal arts curriculum must selectively and purposively be ordered to both knowledge and appreciation, climaxing in intellectual and affective awareness of the highest Source of value. Worship, in this sense, is the teleological fulfillment of a liberal arts education, in Augustine's eyes. Humans are less human when they do not allow the soul to ascend to its Source in praise.

Incarnation and humility

As noted in Chapter 1, Augustine finds a complementary picture of the moral-spiritual goal of divine contemplation in the Platonists, but not a way to get there. They teach him of the eternal *logos* ("Reason" or "Word") who governs cosmic order—but that this *logos* "became flesh and dwelt among us" he finds nowhere in their books.

> In them [the books of the Platonists] I read (not that the same words were used, but precisely the same doctrine was taught, buttressed by many and various arguments) that *in the beginning was the Word, and the Word was with God; he was God. He was with God in the beginning. Everything was made through him; nothing came to be without him. What was made is alive with his life, and that life was the light of humankind* (John 1:1-2) ... But that *the Word was made flesh and dwelt among us* (John 1:14), I did not read there ... [and] that *he emptied himself and took on the form of a slave, and being made in the likeness of men was found in human form,* that *he humbled himself and was made obedient to the point of death, even death on a cross* (Phil. 2:6-11) ... of this not a mention was made in these books [of the Platonists]. (*CF* 7.13-14)

Augustine learns the goal—contemplation of divine *logos*—but not the way. This divine descent of the *logos* in the Incarnation—glimpsed in the prologue to John's gospel (John 1:1-18)—transforms Augustine's sense of contemplation as the moral-spiritual goal of liberal arts education in a few important ways.

Incarnation becomes the symbol of genuine liberal education, for Augustine, wherein the upward intellectual ascent becomes a downward divine descent, an icon of the intellectual virtue of humility. The spiritual goal of education now mysteriously has a personality, a face, a body associated with it. The contemplative consummation of learning is no longer ultimately about ascent, or an escape from the flux of material reality, but rather a descent further into the inherent goodness of material reality and the particularity of creation. Christ is not only the embodiment of the longed-for contemplative vision, but also the demonstration of divine humility wherein the infinite becomes finite, the eternal temporal, and the great and glorious God a lowly baby. The poetry of Incarnation reveals a true path for education—the way toward ultimate height is found in the enfleshed world of vision and touch and desire. Augustine speaks of the virtue of intellectual humility as a kind of "learned ignorance"—a stretching of the soul toward the mysterious truth about God's nature revealed in Christ, who is "Truth in person" (*CF* 7.25).

Augustine's *Confessions* suggests that disordered desire and the perils of self-love haunt liberal education at every stage. His autobiography reveals that disordered love of the intellectual goods of a liberal education may be even more dangerous than the carnal love of material goods. Disordered love of intellectual mastery cultivates the vice of intellectual pride—a form of self-mastery and exclusive trust in the internal authority of one's own reason. Augustine has an illuminationist epistemology, which means that he thinks the human capacity to reason and know truth is made possible by participation in the divine light.[1] It is all too easy to ignore this participation, Augustine thinks, and mistake the diving light for one's private faculty.

Given Augustine's view of human nature—and his anthropology of Trinitarian image-bearing—love of learning actualizes a part of human nature that is central to our uniqueness as divine image-bearers. Due to the effects of original sin in the human soul—and

---

[1] For a helpful overview of Augustine's epistemology in his early writings on liberal education, see Chapter 6. "Authority and Illumination" in Ryan N.S. Topping, *Happiness and Wisdom: Augustine's Early Theology of Education* (Washington, DC: Catholic University of America Press, 2012), 185–226.

the implicit danger of mistaking the internal light of reason as one's own—the fullness of contemplative vision has been hidden from humans. There is no purely intellectual path of ascent from the liberal arts to a vision of God. For unlike intellectual or technical mastery of the material world, divine contemplation is not a goal that can be achieved without the corresponding interior transformation—without properly ordered love—achieved through Christ. Progress in the intellectual life makes one susceptible to the temptation of "presumption"—of being "puffed up with knowledge" rather than built up in the true wisdom found in love. "For I had already begun to covet a reputation for wisdom ... I [was] complacently puffed up with knowledge. Where was that charity which builds on the foundation of humility that is Christ Jesus?" (*CF* 7.26).

> At present I do not contemplate you [God], because I have fallen over; in the time to come I shall stand up and gaze. This is the human cry. The human race has fallen, but had we not fallen the one who was to raise us up would not have been sent. We fell, he came down. He ascended, we are lifted up, because nobody has gone up to heaven except the one who descended. We who came crashing down are lifted up, because he who came down is raised on high. We should not lose hope because he ascended alone, for he raises us up, even us, to whom he descended as we were falling. We shall stand before him and contemplate, and the greatest delight will be ours to enjoy, delight beyond measure. (*EP* 26(2).8)

Prior to Augustine's discovery of the books of the Platonists, he went through a period of devotion to Skepticism. It was this philosophical period of disciplined doubt—of withholding mental assent from all propositions—that purged him of his Manichean "superstition," or what he came to see as a false appeal to religious certainty. This doubt cleared the way for his discovery of the Platonists and the Incarnate Christ. In Manichaeanism, faith functioned as an end-run around the limits of human understanding. In his discovery of Platonism, Augustine regained confidence in reason itself, and this, in turn, enabled him to discover reason's own limits as he was "beaten back." It is at this point—at the point where he has fully extended his reason and can go no further—that he discovers a faithful and reverent awe in the face of the overwhelming intricacy of the world. His intellect has pushed as far as it can go—he peers over the cliff of human understanding—and the First Principle meets him in the face of Christ, offering him a bridge.

> the Word became flesh so that your Wisdom, through whom you created all things, might become for us the milk adapted to our infancy. Not yet was I humble enough to grasp the humble Jesus as my God, nor did I know what his weakness had to teach. Your Word, the eternal Truth who towers above the higher spheres of your creation, raises up to himself those creatures who bow before him; but in these lower regions he has built himself a humble dwelling from our clay, and used it to cast down from their pretentious selves those who do not bow before him, and make a bridge to bring them to himself. (*CF* 7.24)

Divine contemplation is thus achieved, in Augustine's view, in the dual flight of reason (the internal authority of one's own light) and faith (trust in the external authority of the teacher who is Christ). Augustine would agree with Pope John Paul II that faith and reason are the two wings of the soul.[2] What is more, for Augustine, Christ is the power in both wings—the internal light of reason (as eternal *logos*) as well as the teacher in whose witness and testimony one must trust to soar. God's self-revelation in the Incarnation is a completing beauty for Augustine—not an instrument at human disposal but the exemplary, salvific therapy for broken nature. The Incarnation is not only an act of divine power, but a way to be followed—a model to be emulated—in the intellectual life.

---

[2] John Paul II, *Fides et Ratio* (Encyclical Letter). http://w2.vatican.va/content/john-paul-ii/en/encyclicals/documents/hf_jp-ii_enc_14091998_fides-et-ratio.html (accessed April 16, 2017)

[T]he mind itself, even though reason and intelligence dwell in it by nature, is by its dark and inveterate faults made unable not only to embrace and enjoy but even to bear His immutable light until it has been renewed from day to day, and healed, and made capable of such great felicity; and so it had first to be imbued with faith, and so purified. And in order that the mind might walk more confidently towards the truth, the Truth itself, God, God's son, assuming humanity without putting aside His Godhood, established and founded this faith, that man might find a way to man's God through God made man. For this is "the Mediator between God and man: the man Christ Jesus" (1 Timothy 2:5). For it is as man that He is the Mediator and the Way. If there is a way between one who strives and that towards which he strives, there is hope of his reaching his goal; but if there is no way, or if he is ignorant of it, how does it help him to know what the goal is? The only way that is wholly defended against all error is when one and the same person is at once God and man: God our goal, man our way. (*CG* 11.2)

Incarnation teaches another lesson to Augustine that is central to liberal arts education. If it is true that the Highest Good has descended into human form and eternally joined human nature to his own, then God has also become the neighbor—a human being one has been called to love in the second great commandment. In the Incarnation, Augustine glimpses an even tighter connection between intellectual inquiry and moral growth (the order of love) as well as a bridge between contemplative ascent and concrete neighbor love.

Outward ordering: Love of neighbor and liberal education

How does the good of a liberal arts education relate to the second great command to love one's neighbor as oneself? How does one properly order one's love for learning (or the goods of a liberal arts education, more broadly) in such a way that it helps to fulfill not only the first great command but the second also, carrying one out in love for the neighbor?

The ethical use of a liberal arts education

For Augustine, the whole of a liberal arts education is ultimately an instrumental good—a good to be put to good use; not merely in pursuit of academic or career achievement, but in one's pursuit of a happy life and ascent toward God. But how should a liberal arts education be put to good use—that is, be instrumentally ordered— in terms of acquiring the practical economic necessities that make this-worldly life possible and enjoyable? In Augustine's experience, liberal arts education had been too narrowly ordered toward the self-interested aims of career and riches. And the antidote to this inward bent, in Augustine's mind, is found in fulfilling the command to love one's neighbor. The command of neighbor love casts good use of a liberal arts education—and intellectual ascent—in a new light and provides a richer sense of how liberal studies constitutes a unique form of neighbor love.

For Augustine, the liberal arts, like all temporal goods, are ultimately to be loved and put to good use for the sake of friendship— friendship either with God or with other human beings. Friendship, he believes, is an outward-driving process through which we begin with the instinctual drive of self-preservation and self-love as infants (friends with oneself), and slowly this sphere of self-regard extends outward through the concentric circles of social friendship. Essential to Augustine's model of friendship is the idea that each individual's ethically significant relationships are defined by a series of concentric "moral circles" radiating out from the individual's soul by orders of social distance: beginning with the body–soul union (which Augustine calls "health"), on to the household and political community, and ending with distant strangers, the cosmos, and God. There is an implicit moral imperative within his view of friendship: It is praiseworthy to extend the sphere of self-regard as widely as possibly.

A passage from Augustine's *Sermons* summarizes his view of friendship and properly ordered neighbor love:

> The necessary [instrumental] goods in this world amount to these two things: health [*salus*] and a friend. These are the things that we should value highly and not despise. Health and a friend are goods of nature. God made man to be and to live; that's health; but so that he shouldn't be alone, a system of friendship was worked out. So friendship begins with married partner and children, and there moves on to strangers. But if we consider that we all have one father and one mother [Adam and Eve], who will be a stranger? Every human being is neighbor to every other human being. Ask nature, is he unknown? He's human. Is she an enemy? She's human. Is he a foe? He's human. Is she a friend? Let her stay a friend. Is he an enemy? Let him become a friend ... So what is health for you must also be health for your friend. As regards the friend's clothing, "Whoever has two shirts, should share with the one who has none;" as regards the friend's food, "and whoever has food should do likewise" (Luke 3:11). You're fed, you feed; you're clothed, you clothe. (*S* 299D.1-3)

This passage captures the outward drive of Augustine's theory of properly ordered love. Ordered love and proper use of temporal goods always work in two directions: upward and outward.

A liberal arts education is a temporal good that must be put to good use for the sake of tending the forms of friendship—the concentric moral circles and communities—that God has uniquely placed one in and made one responsible for. By cultivating in students the habits of sustained attention to the visible worlds of nature and culture and the disciplines of study—for example, delayed gratification, repeated effort, and failure—a liberal arts education prepares the mind and heart for imagining one's relational responsibility to those far outside the familiar circles. It gives the mind a broader range for compassion's true feeling. One should seek to use one's education in service of the widest circles possible—as wide as one can go without neglecting the narrower circles one is accountable for tending. The skills of critical analysis and communication acquired in study—and the practical abilities mastered in the applied arts—prepare one to meet the necessities of life: needs of safety, order, sustenance, fellowship, liberty, beauty, etc. Such needs remain in the foreground as motivational cause to endure the rigors of a liberal arts education. Yet the world also needs people with adequate soul formation—ones who not only know how to serve and get where they want to go but also know what sort of person they ought to become—able to answer the moral question for education: What should I do? Liberal arts education should cultivate an expansion of one's moral imagination—both in terms of who counts as the neighbor and the ways one can love such a neighbor in the real world.

Learning is thus a gift that not only initiates one into discovery of the mysterious worlds of nature and culture—reality in all of its fullness—but also affords one the opportunity to discover one's own particular capacities for mastering these fields of inquiry, and discerning how that mastery might turn into the applied, productive expression of that discipline as a contribution to the flourishing of the communities in which one finds oneself. Knowledge enables us to serve each other in the ways that matter—keeping children warm, creating beautiful and safe homes, putting food on the table, creating laughter, engaging in lively edifying discussion, etc. This perspective on education and friendship, and the good use of a liberal arts education, turns education into a vocation: a task worthy in its own right and instrumentally ordered toward one's career. It also casts the economic purpose and question of liberal arts education—What shall I make?—in a new light. One's making is meaningful insofar as it meets the physical as well as the intellectual, moral, and spiritual needs of the communities in which one finds oneself. There is an implicit connection between education and one's dual obligations to one's primary affiliations as well as to humanity in the broadest sense.

The study of humanity

Liberal arts education represents a special form of neighbor love in its own right. Careful, patient study of the records and artifacts and monuments of human ingenuity, creativity, and rationality are an expression of attentive longing to understand the world outside of oneself, one's time, one's familiar community, and one's place. This study expands the soul outwardly, horizontally, untangling the knots of disordered desire that tend to curl inwardly—narrowing one's horizon. In this sense liberal education is the study of humanity—the neighbor. This kind of study humanizes one as one begins to recognize the humanity of the neighbor and of oneself in the common inheritance of learning. The curriculum and college classroom play a special role in cultivating the virtue of humanity insofar as the institution uniquely stands at the crossroads of the concentric circles—the household, church, state—and draws one into a community of learners in which one is called to recognize every other human being as the neighbor whom one has been called to love. Liberal arts education ordered toward neighbor love humanizes us, widens our sympathies and spheres of concern.

Humans mysteriously meet God in the neighbor, Augustine says, and simultaneously fulfill the double commandments through neighbor love. The way up, out of the self toward God, is found in the outward way of neighbor love.

> We've all got neighbors; reach out now to the neighbor, in order to love God with whole heart, whole soul, whole mind. O man, "if you do not love the brother whom you can see, how will you be able to

love God whom you cannot see" (1 John 4:20)? Yes, you recognize the words borrowed from the talk of the apostle John. So it gives us a rule to follow: let us start from our neighbor, in order to arrive at God. (*S* 90A.5)

Here the good use of a liberal arts education in loving identification with humanity—and service to that neighbor through one's talents—forms a kind of bridge between love of God and neighbor. One can cross this bridge, in Augustine's eyes, simply by being present to the many everyday tasks—both of liberal education and practical necessity—in which neighbor love consists. Both movements of love—upward and outward—are necessary for properly ordered love within. Only in this horizon can healthy self-love be formed and properly formed love of liberal education be wrought.

3

The Art of Reading

But be doers of the word, and not merely hearers who deceive themselves. For if any are hearers of the word and not doers, they are like those who look at themselves in a mirror; for they look at themselves and, on going away, immediately forget what they were like. But those who look into the perfect law, the law of liberty, and persevere, being not hearers who forget but doers who act—they will be blessed in their doing.

James 1:22-25

We are under-bred and low-lived and illiterate; and in this respect I confess I do not make any very broad distinction between the illiterateness of my townsman who cannot read at all, and the illiterateness of him who has learned to read only what is for children and feeble intellects ... We are a race of tit-men, and soar but little higher in our intellectual flights than the columns of the daily paper.

Henry David Thoreau, *Walden*

Introduction

Why a whole chapter on reading? Reading has long been understood as central to liberal arts education—especially in the humanities—and particularly as it pertains to the pursuit of the moral and spiritual purposes of learning. Reading is a fertile ground for acquiring the habits of mind and heart—for example, attention, self-understanding—constitutive of a well-educated person. The idea is simple: One must become adept at reading good books in order to become a good person. The intrinsic value of this practice has traditionally been understood in terms of self-formation—that is, reading in order to become oneself. Yet this justification requires a normative view of the self that is being formed in order to give the practice meaning. Today—as humanities majors and programs dwindle—there is a pressing need to explain the importance of reading. Beyond its apparent instrumental value for career preparation—that is, the development of transferable critical thinking and communication skills—what justifies the time-intensive practice of reading?

This question feels increasingly out of step in the age of STEM discipline competencies and the instrumentalization of higher education. It is a fundamentally human question—it is about losing touch with (or recovering) the picture of selfhood that has justified reading for millennia. That old picture—which interlocks reading and selfhood—increasingly sounds like moral alchemy, a superstition to be unshackled from in favor of newfound freedom. As technologically driven views of human plasticity and perfectibility gain traction—as Silicon Valley turns out new frameworks for self-design—it is critical to ask anew: What view of the human person is required to sustain the liberal arts? What kinds of people ought the liberal arts produce?

In this chapter, I argue that unless we recover the moral tradition of reading, the humanities—which keep texts and critical human consideration together—will continue to shrivel as they lose student interest and cultural influence. Already, the humanities have tried and failed to keep pace with the research methodology and voluminous output of the natural and social sciences. But this effort has come at the cost of losing sight of the moral and spiritual purposes of reading—that is, of the moral and spiritual *telos* of liberal learning.

Unless we recover a rich understanding of reading's value, the humanities may not survive the current economic crisis apart from a few elite programs that enroll students with an extraordinary amount of resources.

A brief history of liberal education reveals three dominant models of reading and selfhood. First, the Socratic model in which reading fosters self-examination; second, the Augustinian, where reading is self-reception; and third, the Romantic, where reading drives self-creation. It is my goal in this chapter to present the Augustinian model as the most compelling picture of reading—and one that demands recovery. Contemporary college students are stuck between the Socratic and Romantic pictures of self-examination and self-creation. The contemporary college *reader* is stuck between an essential self and the dizzying freedom of inventing oneself. The Augustinian view offers a middle way—between self-examination and self-creation, best described as self-reception. For Augustine, there is no preexistent Platonic soul to be discovered, nor is there an utterly contingent self to be fashioned. Rather the self is both given and made. It's a narrative conception of selfhood, where selves are coauthored with God in the marriage of self-knowledge and knowledge of God. Reading, on this account, is the definitive practice in Christian liberal arts education through which practitioners coauthor and receive their selves.

The Augustinian reader discerns herself and receives selfhood through two contemporaneous linguistic practices—interpreting texts and narrating identity through language. In brief, words are the medium of selfhood. She finds moments of stability and self-understanding by internalizing the written word. Augustine's thought maintains a tension between the human task of moral reading and the spiritually charged task of reading sacred Scripture. This productive tension gave rise to the many different forms of Christian humanism in the late middle ages, Renaissance and Reformation, and early modern period—forging a view of the reader that gave birth to the medieval university and Protestant liberal arts college.

This chapter has three aims: First, to explore Augustine's relation to the philosophical tradition of moral reading; second, to focus on Augustine's view of reading Scripture; and third, to offer a reflection on Augustinian reading as antidote to the present version of late-modern reading and self-creation.

Augustine and the art of moral reading

What is reading? Human beings are reading animals, constantly reading—reading road signs, facial gestures, and tabloids. To read is to interpret. To read is to follow signs to the things that those signs direct one to. What happens within one's mind when one reads? How does a child transition from sounding out letters to deciphering them within the mind, extracting meaning? Learning to read a foreign language as an adult is a beneficial, if painful, reminder of how well-adapted most human beings become at the art of extracting meaning from clusters of letters on a page in a single language. Words are all signs that point toward things. The three letters D-O-G spell "dog" and refer to a thing: the furry four-legged creature.

Why read? There are many different reasons to read—to get a good grade on a test, to be in the know, to find directions, to have something clever to say, to be entertained. What is the purpose of reading itself? Pleasure? Information? Career or intellectual achievement? Assuredly, there are many valid motivations for reading—but is there a moral and spiritual purpose in reading?

As with the physical body, one chooses to feed oneself things that give health and life, but also things that are momentarily pleasurable yet ultimately empty or even damaging. By good habit one shapes one's will to enjoy and acquire taste for the things that give life and health. The life of the mind is fed by the external, the inputs of the senses—predominantly by words and visible images. Reading books connects the internal and external dimensions of life. And reading certain kinds of books is particularly good for the inner person.

Augustine is part of a philosophical tradition that sees reading as integrally bound with moral and spiritual growth—that is, bound with the pursuit of a happy life and divine contemplation.[1] Indeed, the *Confessions* is perhaps the most illuminating book about the habit of reading ever written. In it he shows how intertwined reading was with his pursuit of the happy life and dramatizes his spiritual quest toward God in terms of his journey as a reader. Reading, for Augustine, becomes a metaphor for the spiritual journey and he presents himself as an imperfect exemplar for imitation.

Motivation

The first stage of a reader's moral and spiritual growth concerns motivation. When Augustine was young, he read for entertainment. As he progressed in school, he read for achievement and career ambition. When he finally arrived in Carthage for college, he encountered a book by Cicero called the *Hortensius* that transformed both his motivation for reading as well as his sense of its possibilities for transforming him. The *Hortensius* (unfortunately now lost) is a "protreptic"—an introduction to philosophy and an exhortation to pursue wisdom. The book is a call to attend to oneself, and to turn from the pursuit of external things toward the internal, imperishable good of wisdom.

Augustine reports that, although he encounters Cicero's book in his regular course of studies in the liberal arts, in rhetoric, it was not the book's usefulness or sophistication that drew him in, but rather

---

[1] For an excellent study of Augustine's inheritance of the ancient philosophical tradition of moral reading, see Brian Stock, *Augustine the Reader: Meditation, Self-Knowledge, and the Ethics of Interpretation* (Cambridge, MA: Harvard University Press, 1998).

the urgency of its appeals and the new purpose for education that captivated him:

> Still young and immature, I began in the company of these people to study treatises on eloquence. This was a discipline in which I longed to excel, though my motive was the damnably proud desire to gratify my human vanity. In the customary course of study I had discovered a book by an author called Cicero, whose language is almost universally admired, though not its inner spring. This book of his is called the *Hortensius* and contains an exhortation to philosophy. The book changed my way of feeling and the character of my prayers to you, O Lord, for under its influence my petitions and desires altered. All my hollow hopes suddenly seemed worthless, and with unbelievable intensity my heart burned with longing for the immortality that wisdom seemed to promise. I began to rise up, in order to return to you. My interest in that book was not aroused by its usefulness in the honing of my verbal skills (which was supposed to be the object of the studies I was now pursuing, in my nineteenth year, at my mother's expense, since my father had died two years earlier); no, it was not merely as an instrument for sharpening my tongue that I used that book, for it had won me over not by its style but by what it had to say. How ardently I longed, O my God, how ardently I longed to fly to you away from earthly things! I did not understand then how you were dealing with me. Wisdom resides with you, but love for wisdom is called by the Greek name "philosophy," and this love it was that the book kindled in me. (*CF* 3.7-8)

In the *Hortensius*, Augustine encountered not only a different kind of book (a book that is about wisdom and not mere eloquence or rhetorical sophistication) but a book that motivates a new kind of reading. Augustine's response to this book is intense—almost inexplicably intense, given all he had already experienced in his educational journey up to that point in the narrative—and appears almost as a pre-conversion conversion, signaling the role reading will play in his total spiritual transformation. Cicero's book enflames a love for wisdom which begins his journey back to God—the central plot of the whole autobiographical narrative.

A pagan philosophical text produced the seminal inner change in Augustine. He emphasizes this by turning in the next section of his narrative to recount his inability to read Scripture during his studies at Carthage because the language seemed too lowly and unsophisticated in comparison with Cicero's. He had not yet been formed inwardly to appreciate the humble beauty of the Scriptural text, yet he *had* begun his ascent back to God.

Attention

Good reading requires our attention, for Augustine. Indeed, reading can help us measure how susceptible to distraction we are. How frustrating to come back to oneself and realize that although the eyes have scanned a whole page, one has been elsewhere. Likewise, how satisfying to feel the mind fully engaged in the process of extracting meaning from letter clusters on a page and to be rewarded with understanding. Attention, for Augustine, is the mind's desire. The capacity for sustained attention is a faculty that must be trained and exercised. The soul is prone, in Augustine's view, to live a scattered, fragmented mental life. It would be easy to blame modern technology for this problem, yet the writings of ancients such as Augustine suggest that humans have always had trouble paying attention. For Augustine, reading is a remedy—an exercise through which one can gather his scattered thoughts and bring his self back together. Good reading of good books not only provides the therapy of mental focus but delivers the moral insight that powers self-reception.

Good reading is an antidote to an overly multitasked or distracted life. In good reading the mind should be engaged with the words on the page—sometimes in a dance, sometimes in a wrestling match.

Henry David Thoreau—an inheritor of this tradition of reading as a moral and spiritual exercise—speaks of the strenuousness of the task:

> To read well, that is, to read true books in a true spirit, is a noble exercise, and one that will task the reader more than any exercise which the customs of the day esteem. It requires a training such as the athletes underwent, the steady intention almost of the whole life to this object. Books must be read as deliberately and reservedly as they were written. (*Walden*, 68)

Thoreau says also that other kinds of reading—the ones that do not require sustained attention, mostly done in service of instrumental ends, or what he calls "convenience"—are actually not reading at all:

> Most men have learned to read to serve a paltry convenience, as they have learned to cipher in order to keep accounts and not be cheated in trade; but of reading as a noble intellectual exercise they know little or nothing; yet this only is reading, in a high sense, not that which lulls us as a luxury and suffers the noble faculties to sleep the while, but what we have to stand on tiptoe to read and devote our most alert and wakeful hours to. (*Walden*, 70–71)

One must "stand on tiptoe" to truly read—a "noble intellectual exercise." All the great proponents of this kind of attentive reading—from Seneca to Augustine to Thoreau—lament how schools, the cultural purveyors of books and reading, fail to train in this type of reading. Augustine laments his education throughout *Confessions*, saying his training in words was merely a brutal initiation into the arts of grammar and then style—all utterly divorced from any improvement in the inner life in which the text bears meaning and shapes the self. Thoreau, likewise, offers such lamentations throughout *Walden*, arguing that his new home in the woods was much "more favorable, not only to thought, but to serious reading, than a university" (*Walden*, 67). Thoreau echoes both Augustine and his teacher and friend, Ralph Waldo Emerson. In "The American Scholar," Emerson exhorts college teachers to cultivate students in the real art of reading, noting that it is an "active soul" that makes the difference:

> Books are the best of things, well used; abused, among the worst. What is the one end which all means go to effect? They are for nothing but to inspire. I had better never see a book than to be warped by its attraction clean out of my own orbit, and made a satellite instead of a system. The one thing in the world, of value, is the active soul. ("The American Scholar," 47)

The first author before Augustine to fully articulate the idea of reading as a spiritual and moral exercise—and also to decry how inimical professional liberal arts education can become toward this habit—is the ancient Roman philosopher Seneca. Students are unfortunately trained to read only in order to become smart, not good, according to Seneca: "Attentiveness to words, analysis of syllables, accounts of myths, laying down the principles of prosody? What is there in all this that dispels fear, roots out desire or reins in passion?" (Letter 88). Students read great works by authors such as Homer but their motivation is aimed solely at pleasure, entertainment, career achievement, and intelligence apart from goodness. All of these purposes fall short of the highest purpose for reading. "Are you more concerned to find out where Ulysses' wanderings took him than to find a way of putting an end to our own perpetual wanderings?" Seneca writes to Lucillius (Letter 88). Seneca repeatedly uses the wandering figure of Ulysses (Odysseus) as a central metaphor for the distracted soul—the homesick sojourner—and as a way of dramatizing the role reading plays on the journey home.

In the *Confessions* Augustine models his spiritual memoir on the homebound journeys of Odysseus and Aeneas—and his transformative encounters with books become episodes whereby the wandering wayfarer comes to himself and recognizes his distance from home. Augustine uses the language of wandering and distance—and ideas of returning home and finding port—to convey the strangely dual sense of self-formation found through reading: self-development (sailing) and self-reception (mooring in home port). Books become sails for the winds of the sea, guides to the night sky on the way home to the happy life, to God. This model of sojourning has deep biblical resonance for Augustine as well—the journey of Abraham, the Prodigal Son's return, and the wandering Israelites. Augustine conjoins the Homeric and biblical images with the Platonic view of the world's emanation from the Source of being and its eventual return. Books are like deck hands for setting sail and telescopes for reading navigational clues. They provide substance one must interpret and appropriate along the way. Good reading provides wake-up calls, maps, signposts, and the encouragement necessary to continue.

Joining with Seneca and Augustine, Thoreau narrates his journey at Walden through close reading of Homer: "I kept Homer's *Iliad* on my table through the summer, though I looked at his page only now and then ... I read one or two shallow books of travel in the intervals of my work, till that employment made me ashamed of myself, and I asked where it was that *I* lived" (*Walden*, 67). Here Thoreau plays with the metaphor of traveling by lamenting his wayward desire to read travel books rather than Homer, and suggests that his desire reveals insufficient motivation for reading and a weak capacity for attention. For Seneca, Augustine, and Thoreau there is a strong connection between reading and *travel*—and the metaphor of journeying into the ideas of others by reading must be reconciled with the need for stillness, solitude, and being alone with oneself. There are deeper and more superficial ways to go about reading and traveling—and each requires an open spirit, a combination of self-awareness and self-forgetfulness. The depth of one's engagement in the place or book determines the possibility of inner transformation. Too much travel—or too many books—carried off too quickly diminishes the soul-expansion, self-understanding, and self-recognition available on the journey. For all of these authors, the ability to read and travel well is completed by the ability to be alone in one's own company.

> Judging from what you tell me and from what I hear, I feel that you show great promise. You do not tear from place to place and unsettle yourself with one move after another. Restlessness of that sort is symptomatic of a sick mind. Nothing, to my way of thinking, is a better proof of a well ordered mind than a man's ability to stop just where he is and pass some time in his own company. (Seneca, *Letter* 2)

"[T]earing from place to place" is symptomatic of a sick mind, says Seneca, in an image that becomes central to Augustine's *Confessions*. One cannot help but think of the way contemporary society's art of reading is now connected to the internet by smart phones—an ultimate version of mental travel cleansed of all the gritty otherness and consequences of being in different places and times. "To be everywhere is to be nowhere." But not just any text will help the reader get home, in Seneca's and Augustine's views. The first criterion for the worthiness of a text is whether one's predecessors have deemed it worthy of attention, and whether the text demands and repays sustained efforts of attentive reading.

> Be careful, however, that there is no element of discursiveness and desultoriness about this reading you refer to, this reading of many different authors and books of every description ... To be everywhere is to be nowhere. People who spend their whole life traveling abroad end up having plenty of places where they can find hospitality but no real friendships. (Seneca, Letter 2)

Conscience

A second criterion for discerning the worthiness of a text for moral and spiritual formation is whether or not the text resonates with the conscience, or what Augustine sees as the internal text: "Knowledge of letters lies less deep in us than the law written in our conscience which forbids us to do to another what we would not have done to ourselves" (*CF* 1.29). The wordless inner text is stamped on the soul by God. It is the first standard of judgment. A developing awareness of it, and sensitivity to it, is the most primal kind of reading, for Augustine. Any book worth reading will enliven one to this internal word—acting as an opposing flint, striking and forming the spark of conscience. Conscience, for Augustine, is the first form of moral and spiritual self-knowledge, and good books vivify and make articulate this inner book.

Good books also act as mirrors, for Augustine, in which one glimpses the inner self. This is why Thoreau exhorts one to read in the morning—to "consecrate morning hours to [a good book's] pages"— because it is at this point that the pond is settled and one can see bottom (*Walden*, 68). Bringing the self out *into* the words on the page through the work of interpretation allows one to see and to read the self, giving one inward vision. Presentation of the self to itself through words is akin to conversation with a close friend. In true conversation, one presents oneself to a friend by words—often surprising oneself, catching a glimpse of a part of the self that had remained opaque until drawn forth in language. Part of what it means to "confess," for Augustine, is to recognize that the self is made with words. Augustine wants to confess his whole self to God—and to do so, the *Confessions* suggests, he must search for and find the right words, many of them borrowed from good books.

Textual self-understanding

Self-knowledge comes, in Augustine's eyes, through self-narration. Self-narration is the art of presenting one's life as a narrative—as a "book"—through words addressed to oneself and to God. Reading is thus the joint exegesis of the word and the self. We tirelessly seek understanding of another's words, and in this absorbing act of self-forgetfulness the self appears. If one can find oneself in words, it is because one has been given words that allow her to make sense of her interior landscape. Augustine says: "And what of myself: Where was I as I sought you? You were straight ahead of me, but I had roamed away from myself and could not find even myself, let alone you!" (*CF* 5.2). The truly great texts, such as Cicero's *Hortensius* or "the books of the Platonists," call Augustine to return to himself, and there he finds God. By reading, Augustine becomes increasingly convinced that the self is not in *there*—somewhere in inner space—like an inner pearl waiting to be found, but rather it must be called forth and created by words in conversation with God.

Transformation

Once a reader gains a glimmer of self-understanding, the question becomes: How then shall I live? True reading, for Augustine—like Seneca before him and Thoreau after him—changes one's life. Although the practice is a predominantly inward activity, it must have real bearing on one's practical course of action—not just the way one thinks and feels, but the way one lives. Thoreau remarks, "[i]t is not all books that are as dull as their readers … How many a man has dated a new era in his life from the reading of a book" (*Walden*, 73). A third criterion for discerning the worthiness of a text for moral and spiritual formation is whether the book can inspire formative change in one's life. The external signs of inner change are the only evidence of good reading. Thoreau writes that his sole purpose for reading at Walden was to learn how to act—how to emulate the heroes he found in the best books (*Walden*, 68). Montaigne says the same about his love for Plutarch's *Lives* in his essay, "On Books." One should read not only for self-knowledge but also for action. Reading's role in self-reception is predicated on two kinds of work: inner soul work and outer practical work. Character is sealed at the point where thoughts and ideas and commitments turn to action.

At the climax of Augustine's journey as a reader stands the memorable garden scene in Milan where his spiritual struggle crescendos in an encounter with the letters of Paul. Crushed with anxiety and racked by indecision, Augustine leaves his friend Alypius behind in the courtyard and staggers off, plucking his beard, hugging his knees to his chest, crying like a baby. He is torn about whether to enter the Christian church. This decision is bound up with his decision to abandon his sexual promiscuity and to renounce his career as professor of rhetoric.

The journey neared the shores of its destination:

> It was a journey not to be undertaken by ship, or carriage, or on foot ... for to travel—and more, to reach journey's end—was nothing else but to want to go there, but to want it valiantly and with all my heart, not to whirl and toss this way and that a will half crippled by the struggle, as part of it rose up to walk, while part sank down. (*CF* 8.19)

The reading journey has brought him to the destination's shores but he must now decide, he must now will his way into the promised country of the happy life.

Augustine is too agitated to sit still, too distracted to pay attention. It is in this scattered state that Augustine hears the voice of a child singing, "take up and read." He swears he has heard these lines sung before, like the lines of a song in a schoolyard game, but he cannot remember where. He interprets their meaning as

> nothing other than a divine command to open the Book and read the first passage I chanced upon; for I had heard the story of how Antony had been instructed by a gospel text. He happened to arrive while the gospel was being read, and took the words to be addressed

to himself when he heard, *Go and sell all you possess and give the money to the poor: you will have treasure in heaven. Then come, follow me* (Matthew 19:21), so he was promptly converted to you by this plainly divine message. Stung into action, I returned to the place where still Alypius was sitting, for on leaving it I had put down there the book of the apostle's letters. I snatched it up, opened it and read in silence the passage on which my eyes first lighted: *not in dissipation and drunkenness, nor in debauchery and lewdness, nor in arguing and jealousy; but put on the Lord Jesus Christ, and make no provision for the flesh or the gratification of your desires* (Romans 13:13-14). I had no wish to read further, nor was there need. (*CF* 8.29)

The teachers of this art of reading—for example, Victorinus, Antony, et al.—appear to Augustine in book eight like stacked Russian dolls, many of whom he only hears about secondhand. Each episode in book eight is a story about someone who learns to practice the moral and spiritual exercise of reading by hearing the story of another person who also has learned to read in this transformative way.

This literary pattern highlights Augustine's sense that the capacity for transformative reading is not ultimately—or not exclusively—one's own. The transformative moment is a kind of illumination, participation in a light that both is and is not one's own. Or, to continue Augustine's seafaring metaphor of the soul's journey home, in good reading one finds words, like little boats, that take one across the open water toward the beloved home country. In the garden, Augustine finds a ship in the words of the apostle.

Augustine's reading of Scripture

Augustine's ultimate testimony in his *Confessions* is about the singular importance of Scripture as the book of books. In the end, it is this book that is most conducive to true wisdom: self-knowledge and knowledge of God. How does Scripture uniquely provide this for Augustine? What does Scripture offer Augustine that none of the other great formative texts he encountered offered? The words of Cicero and the Platonists, and many others besides, brought him to the point of his conversion in book eight. What is the uniqueness of Scripture in Augustine's mind, and what sort of reading does it uniquely require? The answer to these questions is central—indeed, of ultimate importance—to the nature of an Augustinian liberal arts education.

Scripture and textual self-understanding

Human beings have word-shaped loves, according to Augustine. This is what struck him looking back on his early education in epic poetry—he felt gratitude for the skills of literacy he acquired yet concern over the ways his passions were shaped by exposure to the stories of the amorous gods (*CF* 1.25). Those stories about the gods left him with a mixed moral picture and disordered affection. His enjoyment of the plays at Carthage offered a new phase of disordered desire—enjoyment of sorrow, or, what Augustine later sees as, self-referential addiction to sadness and tragic emotion (*CF* 3.2). The stories he learned in school and saw on stage ordered his affections, molded his sense of value, and shaped his loves. They amounted to the "flood of human custom" by which human beings learn the density of language—a thick symbolic landscape and cultural world, heavy-laden with values—and pass down a sense of what is worth caring about to the next generation (*CF* 1.25). Learning to read is a gift, in Augustine's mind, but one that comes with the burden of mixed affection. Language is essentially good—but it is a corrupted good: a symbolic and cultural world of disordered desire.

Augustine describes the great malformation of his loves through his education as a reader. First, there was epic poetry in his youth, the shows in college at Carthage, then the treatises on eloquence that sharpened his tongue. Training in word use—the foundation of his liberal arts education and the trivium—led inwardly to disordered desire and outwardly to the will to power. At this early stage, Augustine could not find a way to connect his habits as a reader to the moral and spiritual purposes of liberal education. But that changed when he encountered Cicero's *Hortensius*, which evoked in him a love for the immaterial good of wisdom. He reports: "[It] changed my way of feeling and the character of my prayers to you, O Lord, for under its influence my petitions and my desires altered. All my hollow hopes suddenly seemed worthless" (*CF* 3.7).

His breakthrough encounter with the *Hortensius* inspired Augustine to investigate the Scripture that his mother Monica had been goading him toward from his youth, to see what sort of wisdom and desire-transformation might be available there.

> Accordingly I turned my attention to the holy scriptures to find out what they were like. What I see in them today is something not accessible to the scrutiny of the proud nor exposed to the gaze of the immature, something lowly as one enters but lofty as one advances further, something veiled in mystery. At that time, though, I was in no state to enter, not prepared to bow my head and accommodate myself to its ways. My approach then was quite different from the one I am suggesting now: when I studied the Bible and compared it with Cicero's dignified prose, it seemed to me unworthy. My swollen pride recoiled from its style and my intelligence failed to penetrate to its inner meaning. Scripture is a reality that grows along with little children, but I disdained to be a little child and in my high-and-mighty arrogance regarded myself as grown up. (*CF* 3.9)

Scripture—like the Incarnation itself—provides an antidote to the intellectual disease of pride, for Augustine. It first challenges his conception of what counts as a beautiful, intellectual, sophisticated, or important text. It appears inferior in comparison with Cicero's dignified prose. He says that his "swollen pride recoiled from its style" and that the reality of Scripture demanded him to "bow" as he entered, to stoop, to become as a little child in order to enter its lofty halls of meaning, veiled in mystery. Scripture is a book for perpetual beginners, in Augustine's eyes, a book for those who reckon insight and understanding not as an achievement but as a gift. Augustine says that he could not yet "accommodate" himself to its ways—either in terms of intellectual humility to wrestle with its knots and puzzles, or in terms of adapting the moral texture of his life to meet its high demands.

The plainness of the Bible and the childlikeness of those who would approach it should not be misunderstood in terms of relative ease or superficiality of interpretation. On the contrary, in Augustine's view, the Scriptures are and will always remain quite difficult to interpret. The Scriptures exercise the mind and heart; some parts should only be taken literally, other parts only figuratively, and some parts both; some parts of Scripture are obscure and difficult to square with other parts. Some parts of the Bible seem quite grotesque and repugnant, other parts breathtaking in their moral exaltation. All of this presses the intellect to its limits and presses the reader's patience; it stretches the soul. Adequate understanding of this unique text is nothing other than the work of drawing near and contemplating its subject matter: the Word himself. Interpretive understanding thus requires a total commitment of one's mind and heart and conversion of life.

Augustine's strategy for interpreting the great and difficult passages of Scripture is always to look for the Word, Jesus Christ, in them. The whole drift of Scripture is the self-communicating speech-act of God in the humble signs of words. This is yet again a movement of Incarnation for Augustine. God, the inexpressible, empties himself in the feebleness of alphabet and text. This self-communication of the divine climaxes in the event of the Word made flesh (John 1:14).

The message of the Incarnation is both the message of divine love to the world and the sacrifice for sin—as well the concrete self-communication of God. The divine descent of Incarnation is a model of intellectual humility—God allows himself to be coded and revealed in the gestures of human speech. The Incarnation is a symbol that is also the thing it symbolizes. What else can a truly great book do than incarnate its own ideas—to embody its own wisdom in the flesh of its readers?

For Augustine, the great book of Scripture—veiled in mystery and obscurity—must be read in relation to the rule of faith (the central elements of Christian doctrine taught in the Apostle's Creed) and in light of the ethical commands to love God and neighbor. Inscribed within the Scripture's enigmas lie the great moral and spiritual purpose of education—the call to ordered harmony with God, self, and neighbor.

Psalm-shaped self-understanding

After Augustine's conversion in the garden at Milan, he retired to the villa at Cassiciacum where he set to work on his Christian liberal arts curriculum and immersed himself in the Bible. Unlike the playful reading scene in the garden at the end of book eight, in book nine, one finds Augustine practicing a steady, patterned, daily regimen of Psalm recitation within his learning community. "I read the psalms of David," Augustine says, "songs full of faith, outbursts of devotion, with no room in them for the breath of pride" (*CF* 9.8). If Cicero's *Hortensius* had changed his way of feeling and altered his desires, the Psalms set his love on fire for the highest good: "Uncouth I was in real love for you ... How loudly, I began to cry out to you in those psalms, how I was inflamed by them with love for you and fired to recite them to the whole world, were I able, as a remedy against human pride" (*CF* 9.8).

Reading and reciting the Psalms in community offered Augustine a therapy for disordered desire. This therapy transpired as he learned to speak the words as his own—achieving true self-understanding and reforming his deepest desires by them: "I uttered words of my own, interspersed with yours [God] ... I conversed with myself and addressed myself in your presence" (*CF* 9.8). His change of feeling was dramatic: "I read ... [and] I shuddered with awe ... I read on and on, all afire" (*CF* 9.11). "As I read these words outwardly and experienced their truth inwardly," Augustine writes, "I shouted with joy, and lost my desire to dissipate myself amid a profusion of earthly goods, eating up time as I was myself eaten by it; for in your eternal simplicity I now had a different *wheat and wine and oil* (Psalm 4:8)" (*CF* 9.10). It is Augustine's experience with the Psalms that transforms his desire and opens his eyes to the moral and spiritual purpose of reading and leads him to renounce his career: "When the holidays were over I announced my retirement. The citizens of Milan would have to provide another word-peddler for their students" (*CF* 9.13).

The Psalms inflame Augustine's love for God, giving it fresh words, making this love articulate for the first time, giving him words to say to God. The Psalms provide the whole gambit of speech that one might like to say before God—lament, exultation, rage, confession, gratitude, anger, and praise—and thus provide the vehicle by which the finite language user's soul can make its approach. Augustine's *Confessions* are the result of his Psalm-shaped self-understanding. From the opening lines—"Great are you, O Lord, and exceedingly worthy of praise"—the work is an expression of self-understanding achieved and received through the words of the Psalms. Augustine receives himself in the words of the Psalmist.

This experience with the Psalms is a microcosm of Augustine's view of reading Scripture as a whole. Reading Scripture is the central practice in an Augustinian liberal arts education through which one can receive oneself in conversation with God. It is a foretaste of genuine happiness and the gateway to divine contemplation. The mind is a swarm of noisy phantasms, Augustine says, therefore it is no wonder that when one tries to imagine the self or God they are prone to vanity or idolatry. The words of Scripture—and decisively the Word made flesh—are the fix for this predicament. The words provide the vessels and the symbols by which the mind ascends back to God.

Scripture and self-narration

Augustine knew that knowledge of God is inextricably bound with knowledge of oneself. The Delphic maxim "know thyself"—rehearsed time and again by Socrates in Plato's dialogues—is particularly challenging, in Augustine's eyes, because the self is opaque, a knotty tangle of desires, stemming from an inherited problem that goes back all the way to Eden. "I have become an *enigma* even to myself!," Augustine cries in *Confessions* (10.50). Augustine offers his *Confessions* as a grand narrativization of the journey toward true wisdom: knowledge of God and knowledge of oneself. The way to find this wisdom is by inserting oneself—and the memory of one's life—into the grand narrative of God's story given in Scripture: by reading oneself into Scripture.

In the *Confessions*, Augustine is a character in his own story trying on the characters of Scripture. He attempts to know himself first as Adam, created by God in the garden, good and fallen (*CF* 2.9). He envisions himself as David in the great penitential Psalms (*CF* 9.8). He understands himself as the Prodigal Son, wayward and wayfaring, but also beloved and welcomed home by his father (*CF* 1.28). He wants to read and to be read by the words of Scripture. Augustine reinterprets his own past—the thirty-one years leading up to his conversion in the garden at Milan—in light of the Scriptural past so that he can make sense of his present life and shape his expectation and hope for the future. He takes his whole self to Scripture—skeletons, secrets, honest questions, grim doubts, anxieties, and all—so that he can know and understand its truth: a truth that both cuts and comforts. He seeks transformation by Scriptural truth that spans experience, intellect, imagination, and feeling.

Such textual self-understanding is the richest form of self-knowledge, revealed in the mirror of Scripture. Brimming with repentance and praise, lamentation and rage, thanks and jealousy—confession acknowledges the fullness of truth before oneself and God. Augustine discovers this power in Scripture and thus finds himself able to gather his own fragmented, fickle self and to present himself fully before God. There is no way beyond the self, Augustine says, except through the self. "Out of love for loving you, Lord, I do this ... I will try now to give a coherent account of my disintegrated self, for when I turned away from you, the one God, and pursued a multitude of things, I went to pieces" (*CF* 2.1).

Augustine presents his life in the *Confessions* as an example to follow and imitate in the difficult work of achieving Scriptural self-understanding. *Confessions* presents a path toward whole selfhood oriented toward the true goal, true fulfillment, and true completion in God. "Our hearts are unquiet until they find rest in You" (*CF* 1.1). This view of Scriptural self-understanding is the core of the Augustinian view of reading as self-reception.

Recovering the Augustinian view of reading as self-reception

One of the challenges in forming a coherent view of reading and selfhood today is the emphasis on a necessary plurality of texts, methods of reading, and selves that might be deemed worthy of approaching and pursuing. This attempt to recognize all books—without the criteria of determinate moral and spiritual traditions—often results in the predicament of unfenced sheep, clustered around one another in a large pasture. There is no plot line for the self to begin the work of self-narration. Truly liberating self-knowledge is found, for Augustine, in the texts and forms of reading that have been handed down as worthy by one's moral and spiritual predecessors. Reading is by nature first a constraining act—defined by the borders of another's thoughts and power to express—and second a liberation by which one learns to locate oneself within the text and establish one's voice as a member in the great conversation. Augustinian reading is an apprenticeship in soulcraft that provides an opening, a way toward becoming an inheritor of the history of important ideas and a competent judge of the new books that should be included in this canon.

Another challenge in forming a coherent view of reading and selfhood today is the postmodern view of the self that reigns in many versions of liberal education. The enthusiasm and optimism of the Enlightenment's rationalist approach to self-knowledge gave way to a Romantic celebration of genius and universal access to morality and spirituality by intuition and feeling. This Romantic view slowly eroded into a postmodern celebration of subjectivism—a view of the reader as unshackled from the past and committed to the endless play of interpretation and self-creation. This view of reading as self-creation has now merged with a late modern view of freedom as free choice wherein the art of reading becomes a venture of self for pleasurable information, entertainment, or instrumental career development. The instrumentalist defense of liberal arts education supports this view of reading and selfhood wherein the human person is the malleable, self-created self.

As mentioned in Chapter 1, the Augustinian Christian vision of liberal arts education requires a conception of tradition—and the authority of tradition—as an extended conversation about the moral and spiritual purposes of life extended through time. Modernity's revolutionary attempt to overthrow the past and its authoritative texts has resulted in a weakening of selfhood and the moral grammar that has guided our shared conceptions of the good life and good society. One still senses the remnants of this vocabulary—in words such as justice and dignity—yet there is an increasingly thin sense of the content of such concepts. One does not need a better dictionary but rather needs to become a better reader in order to have firsthand encounters with the texts that inaugurate and develop such concepts—whether in poetry, story, philosophy, theology, or any other genre. One also needs a corresponding community of disciplined conversation (constrained agreement and disagreement) about such concepts where one can learn to put them into practice— trying to fit and form content to the work of daily life and learning.

This view of linguistic moral formation through reading is the very center of Augustine's view of reading and selfhood. To have a shared dialogue about the moral and spiritual purposes of liberal arts education—and human life more broadly—requires that a society read and discuss the same books. Listen to any presidential address after a national crisis or celebration. The exalted language is rich with concepts (e.g., the dignity of being made in the image of God, love for humanity, justice for all) that can only be understood by recognizing the moral and spiritual inheritance of the culture expressed in books. What does it mean to have a society that no longer detects such references or knows their histories? Perhaps the distance and distraction of screen-mediated life is making this kind of reading and communion scarce. The need to renew this view of reading as selfhood is urgent. It can be practiced in the college classroom as well as a myriad of other communities—neighborhoods, churches, schools, clubs, and many other associations. Reading in search of oneself, in Augustine's view, requires reading in communion. As in the case of liberal arts education more generally, for Augustine the way toward inner order is the way up and the way out. Texts spark this movement.

4

Citizenship

Introduction

Every educational system aims to produce not only a certain kind of human being but a certain kind of citizen. This understanding of education is at the core of the liberal arts tradition and goes back to its very beginnings in ancient Greece and Rome. As noted in Chapter 1, according to Plato and Aristotle there is a double-*telos* or purpose at the heart of education: On the one hand, education fits us for our highest fulfillment as human beings in truthful contemplation of reality itself and its source in the divine. On the other hand, education suits us for the practical and urgent matter of becoming good members of human society—that is, it makes us good citizens. Thus according to Aristotle, the intellectual virtues acquired through education prepare us ultimately for contemplation, whereas the moral virtues fashion us into just citizens. This second sense of purpose was glimpsed at the end of Chapter 2 in Augustine's view of the outward movement of liberal education in neighbor love. Thus when we talk about liberal arts education in the Western tradition, we are always talking about forming citizens. Indeed, the term *liber*-al arts comes from *liber* in Latin, which can be translated as citizen, or free person. Thus we are not only educating a free person freed for the good life, but an inhabitant of a political community to which the acquired habits of mind and heart will contribute.

What is the good society for which liberal education forms its student-citizens? We need a reasonably coherent view to guide our practice of liberal education. Do we have such a view today? Increasingly, we are stuck between a view of education and citizenship in narrowed nationalism rooted in nostalgia, or a pie-in-the-sky hollow, global cosmopolitanism. The first understanding of citizenship and education exudes a triumphalist streak in terms of the story that it tells about Western civilization and the inheritance of a liberal arts education. The second trades on a marriage of suspicion and deconstructive cynicism that seeks to rework and refit the liberal arts tradition into a broader network of global citizenship—which turns out to be an expansion of liberal democracy and capitalism in the utopic global village. Neither view provides a coherent view of citizenship, and yet both get at something important. The first appreciates the goodness of Western civilization in terms of the political institutions that have emerged from the tradition. The other speaks to the need to transcend narrowed nationalism through a conception of shared humanity—and such a concept is at the heart of the liberal arts tradition and Western civilization. One view cultivates a sense of uniqueness, preservation, and exclusivity in the tradition of liberal education, and the other cultivates a sense of unlimited boundaries, progress, and the universal applicability of liberal education and democracy. Is there a way forward for education and citizenship beyond this impasse?

As in previous chapters, I want to reexamine and explore Augustine's view of liberal education and in this case present his view of citizenship as a way beyond these two options. Augustine's vision of citizenship and education was at the heart of the medieval university and birth of the modern liberal arts college and merits reconsideration in the present moment, for it provides a way that reconciles the twin impulses of triumphalism and cynicism—of local loyalty and global identity.

Augustine's view of citizenship

After his baptism, Augustine moved back home to Roman North Africa to found an alternative Christian liberal arts commune—akin to the one at Cassiciacum—but was then ordained as a priest and bishop, somewhat against his will, because of his intellectual and rhetorical powers. After his ordination he asked for a special dispensation to immerse himself in the study of Scripture in preparation for his new vocation. The sacred text played a vital role in his thought during this period, exerting a pivotal influence on his moral imagination. And after the sack of Rome in 410 AD one biblical trope stands out to Augustine and becomes an ever-present image in his writings, especially in his magnum opus *The City of God* (413–426 AD): the idea of the "other city," and a different kind of citizenship required to become a member of this spiritual and political community. Once Augustine recognized this biblical trope, it appeared to him everywhere: in the typological fulfillment of Jerusalem as the holy city, the "city of God" found throughout the Psalms, the city to which Abraham sojourns in the book of Hebrews, and the "new Jerusalem," the iconic closing image of the Bible in Revelation. Augustine also notes that membership in this other city is expressed in the Roman language of citizenship by the Apostle Paul (e.g., Ephesians 2:19, Philippians 3:20). Indeed, for Augustine, just as the ethical vision of the Bible can be summarized in the twin commandments of love, the whole narrative arc of Scripture is ultimately reducible to these two things: God and the founding of this other city.

This new view of citizenship, on Augustine's account, challenges the ultimacy of our more limited forms of citizenship and political reality. Discovering the other city subordinated Augustine's identification with Roman citizenship and gave him a new critical vantage from which to think about the relationship between liberal arts education and the formation of Roman citizens. Augustine was well positioned to discover this connection between education and citizenship because he had formerly been the imperial professor of rhetoric in Milan at the time of his conversion. Indeed, the crowning liberal art of rhetoric—the culmination of the trivium—represented the fusion of intellectual formation and political identity in service of a good society.

For Augustine, the connection between liberal education and citizenship primarily has to do with the national stories we teach our children in school. Such stories, or founding narratives, provide the linguistic, cultural, moral, spiritual, and political values that cultivate identification with the political community. There is no Babylon without Gilgamesh, no Greece without Homer, and no Rome without Virgil. The Bible presents Augustine with a very different identity-founding narrative world. Indeed, the story of Jesus Christ and the formation of the Christian community in the New Testament—which early Christians understood as the completion and fulfillment of Israel's founding narrative in Exodus—entails a different understanding of the relationship between political society and the spiritual realm. Although many, if not all, other ancient narratives include a sense of transcendence—a realm of gods and spirits that shape political life—the New Testament presented Augustine a different relationship between God and temporal political life. The kingdom of heaven that Augustine discovers in the New Testament is different from Rome both in terms of the exercise of political authority and the kinds of virtues required of its citizens—and this other kingdom's citizens should maintain a kind of ambivalence toward all other political loyalties.

In *The City of God* Augustine performs a critical dialogue between the words of Scripture and the founding literature of Rome—the texts that Augustine took to be most definitive of the ethics of citizenship. By the "ethics of citizenship," I mean the broad sense of narrative-construed political identity that is forged from within the canonical stories, founding myths, heroes, and philosophies most indispensable for a people's shared identity. There is a productive tension at the heart of Augustine's *City of God*: an empathetic appreciation of "the gold of the Egyptians" (Augustine's metaphorical term for the riches of pagan learning in Greek and Roman letters that he borrows from Plato,

Cicero, and others; see *CT* 2.60-61), conjoined with a withering, pull-no-punches critical analysis of the spirit of pagan learning, aimed at unmasking the corrupt moral vision that animates such texts. The opening lines of *The City of God* set the stage. There Augustine brings the two key founding narratives, the Bible and Virgil, into comparative analysis.

> I know, however, what efforts are needed to persuade the proud how great is that virtue of humility which, not by dint of any human loftiness, but by divine grace bestowed from on high, raises us above all the earthly pinnacles which sway in this inconstant age. For the King and Founder of this City of which we are resolved to speak has revealed a maxim of the divine law in the Scriptures of His people, where it is said, "God resisteth the proud but giveth grace unto the humble" (James 4:6). But the swollen fancy of the proud-spirited envies even this utterance, which belongs to God, and loves to hear the following words spoken in its own praise: "To spare the humble and subdue the proud" (Virgil, *Aeneid* 6:853). (*CG* 1.1)

There the spirit of the two cities appears in stark contrast—one founded through lowliness before God, the other in trying to be like God by subduing the proud and sparing the conquered. Is Aeneas' journey and the founding of Rome the most important story in the world? Or is it Christ's way of humility?

For Augustine, liberal education requires historical imagination of the purposive arc of human civilization—an arc that can be detected in the intellectual and literary trail that has come down to us through the ages. Where is the arc going? Where are we in the arc? Which is more important, the rise of the Roman Empire, or the birth of Jesus Christ? This is the question that Scripture poses, and Augustine recognizes that sensitivity to story makes all the difference for the coherence of the education cultures provide their youth and for the kinds of citizens educational systems produce. We only learn to speak by the words we receive, and these stories give us our deepest sense of human and political purpose. Who gets to narrate the world? The answer to that question, Augustine says, is the educators.

The task of a Christian educator, then, is to bring all of the stories of human civilization into fruitful and critical dialogue with Scripture.

> The City of God of which we speak is that to which the Scriptures bear witness: the Scriptures which, excelling all the writings of all the nations in their divine authority, have brought under their sway every kind of human genius, not by a chance motion of the soul, but clearly by the supreme disposition of providence. For it is there written: "Glorious things are spoken of thee, O city of God" (Psalm 87:3). And in another psalm we read: "Great is the Lord, and greatly to be praised in the city of our God, in the mountain of His holiness, increasing the joy of the whole earth" (Psalm 48:1). And a little later in the same psalm: "As we have heard, so have we seen in the city of the Lord of hosts, in the city of our God. God has established it for ever" (Psalm 48:8). And again in another: "There is a river the streams whereof shall make glad the city of our God, the holy place of the tabernacles of the Most High. God is in the midst of her, she shall not be moved" (Psalm 46:4). From these testimonies—and there are others of the same kind, but it would take too long to mention them all—we have learned that there is a city of God, whose citizens we long to be because of the love with which its Founder has inspired us. (*CG* 11.1)

In *The City of God,* Augustine presents himself as the educator, demonstrating how to read pagan texts critically in the light of Scripture, learning how to evaluate their relative merits, and learning how to bring them into conversation with the view of life found in Scripture. The ultimate upshot of the Bible, for Augustine, is the story of *two* cities, diametrically opposed, and two types of citizens, formed by two different types of love. The two loves result from two primordial moral dispositions: pride and humility.

The arc of history bends toward divine judgment, when human beings will be judged on the basis of their interior moral dispositions and delivered to their final ends—eternal happiness or condemnation. The two cities have two founding rulers. Christ, the founder and ruler of the heavenly city, requires that we climb aboard the lowly ship of his cross and make our journey through humility to the eternal city. The other city's ruler and founder is the devil, the first creature to ascend the prideful tower of self-assertion to the exclusion of love for God.

This Augustinian view of ultimate destiny puts the mundane work of politics and education into the sobering horizon of eternity— articulated so clearly in C. S. Lewis's essay, "The Weight of Glory."

It is a serious thing to live in a society of possible gods and goddesses, to remember that the dullest most uninteresting person you can talk to may one day be a creature which, if you saw it now, you would be strongly tempted to worship, or else a horror and a corruption such as you now meet, if at all, only in a nightmare. All day long we are, in some degree helping each other to one or the other of these destinations. It is in the light of these overwhelming possibilities, it is with the awe and the circumspection proper to them, that we should conduct all of our dealings with one another, all friendships, all loves, all play, all politics. There are no *ordinary* people. You have never talked to a mere mortal. Nations, cultures, arts, civilizations— these are mortal, and their life is to ours as the life of a gnat. But it is immortals whom we joke with, work with, marry, snub, and exploit—immortal horrors or everlasting splendors.[1]

Augustine's distinction between the two kinds of ultimate citizens stands beneath every other political distinction we might make about human beings, whether according to nation, class, race, sex, or any other particularity. The formation of our loves produces citizenship in

---

[1] C. S. Lewis, *The Weight of Glory and Other Addresses* (New York: Touchstone/Simon & Schuster, 1996), 39.

one of the two cities—one by excessive self-love leading to the exclusion of God and neighbor; the other by love for neighbor and God, which includes healthy self-love, ordered toward self-transcendence.

> Two cities, then, have been created by two loves: that is, the earthly by love of self extending even to contempt of God, and the heavenly by love of God extending to contempt of self. The one, therefore, glories in itself, the other in the Lord; the one seeks glory from men, the other finds its highest glory in God, the Witness of our conscience … In the Earthly City, princes are as much mastered by the lust for mastery as the nations which they subdue are by them; in the Heavenly, all serve one another in charity, rulers by their counsel and subjects by their obedience. The one city loves its own strength as displayed in its mighty men; the other says to its God, "I will love Thee, O Lord, my strength" (Psalm 18:1). (*CG* 14.28)

It is important to note that, for Augustine, these two cities are ultimate realities and destinations, neither of which can be wholly identified with temporal political society or religious community. There is no clear equivalency between Heavenly or Earthly City and church or state. For Augustine, real political and religious communities are populated by citizens of both moral-spiritual identities, each on their respective pilgrimages to their ultimate destinations. Lest we imagine this story as some rigidified social duality of the in and out, we must remember Augustine's strong sense of the mixture of the two kinds of citizen in the present age (*CG* 11.1), and his acknowledgment of human imperfection and struggle that haunts even the most devoted followers of Christ.

The two cities hermeneutic

Two cities. Two loves. Two interior dispositions and two ultimate destinations. This is the basis of Augustine's tale of two cities and it provides him an interpretive lens—a hermeneutic—by which he reads all of Scripture and the records of human civilization. The spiritual truth of the two cities has many tiers, many layers, and it speaks of our many loves, ranging from mundane cultural goods and entertainment to the profound order of our deepest affections for spouse, country, and ultimately God. *The City of God* performs its own argument. The Bible itself is the story of two cities and provides Augustine the hermeneutical key by which to read all of the other stories of Roman civilization. Everything comes back to the razor of the two cities hermeneutic and the competing formations of love presented in each. The question of what kind of love is being formed and shaped and produced in the reader is the question and basis for judgment of any text. This is the form of literary criticism that Augustine invents in *The City of God*.

What Augustine says elsewhere about good and bad loves and character formation is equally applicable to the questions of citizenship and the formation of societies. Political communities have "common objects of love," and these loves are formed and reinforced by the mega-stories that we tell ourselves about our communities, our origins, and our futures (*CG* 19.24). Augustine's model of literary criticism in *The City of God* is thus also a form of social criticism. Societies are gathered together by these common objects of love in better and worse ways. Some societies have shared love for material goods only, and such societies are continually prone to devolve into disordered desire, decay, mere entertainment, and the perpetual desire to dominate others, both within the society and outside. Another sort of society has shared loves for both material goods *and* the internal goods of virtue—the excellences of character that involve moments of self-transcendence, fellow-feeling, loyalty, and self-sacrifice. Yet these virtues remain unstable (veering back toward the self) unless they are ultimately ordered above the community toward God, who is the Source of true virtue. Without this transcendent horizon, for

Augustine, virtues ultimately result in self-praise or socially conferred glory and the pride of self-mastery. Another form of society has a shared love for God that transcends their love for both material goods and human virtues and thus acquires eternal goods. Common love for God requires a mutual awareness of God as the transcendent Source of value and shared need for help from God to sustain the well-being of the community in this life and the next. The church is the society that, for Augustine, should strive to cling to God as its singular common object of love.

Augustine conceived of the Roman Empire as the first type of society—consumed with material goods—and he thinks that it is this kind of society that predominates the history of civilization. Human nature is prone to be mastered by its own deformed desires and is in turn prone to manipulate and master others in a kind of revenge on its own impotence. Thus, one of the main stories, indeed one of the only two stories, in the world is the story of *pride* as the manifestation of a lust for domination that exudes from those who have already been dominated by their own weakness of will, and are slaves to their passions. Good citizenship and membership in the heavenly city requires clear-eyed self-criticism—which Augustine calls the confession of sin—coupled with an awareness of all the subtle forms of lust for mastery at the level of the individual's soul and society.

In this sense, Augustine is the first deconstructionist—the first master of suspicion—for he reads the Roman rhetoric of political glory as the mask of political arrogance and violence. On his account, there can be no true justice or truly just society in history apart from Christ who is the Ruler and Founder of the heavenly city. Thus human political communities all find themselves on a great spectrum of graded shades of injustice. This sense of suspicion is perfectly expressed in his retelling of the encounter between Alexander the Great and a band of pirates.

It was a pertinent and true answer which was made to Alexander the Great by a pirate whom he had seized. When the king asked him what he meant by infesting the sea, the pirate defiantly replied: "The same as you do when you infest the whole world; but because I do it with a little ship I am called a robber, and because you do it with a great fleet, you are an emperor." (*CG* 4.4; here Augustine is quoting from Cicero's *De republica* 3.14, 24)

Augustine's suspicion of the lust for political domination, coupled with his deep sense of suspicion of the self, keeps a kind of self-critical limit on the deconstructive edge of his social criticism. He has a strong sense of human complicity with evil and sin—including his own. Self-criticism is thus essential for social criticism in his two cities hermeneutic.

Even when our understanding of liberal arts education stretches out to include formation in political virtues such as justice, we cannot transcend the temporal horizon of political glory. Our virtues aim at social recognition by the political community. But virtue, in Augustine's mind, cannot survive within the circularity of socially conferred glory. Even in moments of true self-transcendence and self-sacrifice, Augustine says, we are unable to move into the terrain of true virtue, acting for an end that transcends ourselves. Self-praise vitiates and defeats true virtue. What Augustine speaks of as an "eternal good" is a good (a virtue or a temporal good) that is appropriately employed and directed toward its source in God by gratitude and thus makes us suitable for eternal citizenship in the eternal city—which should be the aim of ultimate learning. But how would we know about the city? First, by Scripture and the witness of the Incarnation. But secondarily in an ongoing way through the appearance of the inhabitants of the eternal city in time, paradigmatically in the martyrs. For they are those who in an almost tragic ray of brilliance reveal self-sacrificing and self-consuming love for God and neighbor, which is the heart of true eternal citizenship.

The City of God is thus Augustine's attempt to locate both the individual human and human civilization within the narrative framework of the origin, descent, and future of humankind—as that history is narrated in Scripture. The Bible is the narrative in reference to which all other stories, memories, histories—both collective and individual—ultimately make sense. This history is the story of creation, fall, and redemption. Like *Confessions*, in which Augustine brings the memory of his own life *into* the narrative of Scripture under the guidance of the Holy Spirit, *The City of God* is Augustine's attempt to bring Roman cultural memory—the repository of accumulated knowledge in texts and practices transmitted through education— into and under the story of Scripture.

The City of God is the culmination of Augustine's project in the Christian liberal arts that he began at Cassiciacum and a manifesto for his view of the curricular content in the language arts (trivium) and humanities. *The City of God* performs the first-ever Christian great books program. For Augustine, human society's cultural memory of past, present, and future is primarily encoded in the biblical books from Genesis to Revelation, and genuine education must bring all other cultural memories into and under the sway of this divinely authoritative one.

Beyond triumphalism and cynicism

Augustine finds a way beyond the twin dangers of cultural triumphalism on the one hand and cynicism on the other. Our tendency to read the past as a self-legitimating story about the virtues of the present age that fuels varieties of narrow nationalism, patriotic nostalgia, or even in our own day a kind of ethno-nationalism must be resisted at all costs. For Augustine, this tendency is understandable. It is an expression of our human proclivity for rose-colored renarration of our cultural past and a way of narrating the achievements of civilization in a way that defends the present order. Yet it is only one more manifestation of the primordial disposition of pride: self-deception. Scripture opens the critical vantage onto our ongoing struggle with being dominated by lust and the lust to dominate others. To do history—to tell the story of the past from the present—requires that we confess our individual and collective sins. To be truthful about a nation's or civilization's history is to remember the darkest elements of demonizing self-interest, domination, injustice, denial, and self-delusion as well as what has been good and is worth preserving. The two are mixed together. There is no other worthy way to tell the story. Long before modernity's perfected art of suspicion for sublimated base motivations in the work of Friedrich Nietzsche and others—a view that sees all of political life and language as a series of power plays and the will to power—there was Augustine, the bishop of Hippo, discovering suspicion's germ of truth in the pages of Scripture.

Yet, for Augustine, suspicion is not license for cynical alienation or resignation but a recipe for deeper self-criticism, deeper identification with the shared weakness of one's social group, and grateful appreciation for the gifts of thought and culture that make the present form of political society possible. His writings present measured gratitude for the "gifts of the pagans," which today we might call the gifts of modern liberal society, as gifts that need to be put to good use. For Augustine, the city of God project is unending, and any human canon, beyond the canon of Scripture, is ultimately unfinished, a work in progress. The story of the two cities, and the hermeneutical lens of pride and humility that it provides, creates the critical vantage from which we can discern the movement of the Holy Spirit in our own secular age. For Augustine, we might also speak of the two cities hermeneutic as a hermeneutic of charity: allowing one to recognize the darkest shadows while also allowing one to identify and redeem what is good.

Finding a way beyond triumphalism and cynicism may be the most pressing question in contemporary liberal arts education, especially in the humanities. Is there a way to restore a hermeneutic of charity in our critical reception of the canon of great works? We are at an impasse between those devoted to an increasingly triumphalist reading of the canon and those devoted to an increasingly cynical resistance to it. The latter position amounts not merely to a rejection of the triumphalist tone of the proponents of the history of Western ideas but a total and complete evacuation of its content, deeming it as unworthy and unfit for the attention of students. If we cannot find a way beyond the impasse, this may spell the end of Western liberal arts education as we have known it.

The Augustinian student must search for injustice within and without through a searching and fearless moral self-inventory, taking responsibility for evil and the sin of self-interest. This theory of self-examination and social criticism falls apart and fails without an appeal to a transcendent ground beyond self and society. The moment of confession, for Augustine, is never a straight arrow of single-minded guilt, but rather a moment of self-clarity that can simultaneously recognize all the external factors and circumstances that might mitigate responsibility—all the wounds and injustice suffered—and yet see through all of these and still claim responsibility for one's own action or inaction. The evil is not *out there*, as it was for Manichean dualists, but rather always out there and in here. This is what it means to stand before God, according to Augustine, and this is what it means to confess one's sin. To be properly trained in the two cities hermeneutic is to find a way between triumphalism and cynicism through the doubled suspicion of internal and external injustice, of self and social criticism, in the confession of sin.

Secularity and citizenship

According to Augustine we live in a secular age—the penultimate age of human history just before the end of time. We are, for Augustine, "time-bound" in the sense that we have no way of knowing how close to the end we are, only that it is imminent. The secular, in Augustine's Latin, denotes this "time-boundedness" and pertinence to this present "age" (*saeculum*). The secular is not a nonreligious space of neutrality but rather a time of the entanglement of the two cities on their way toward their eternal destinations in heaven or hell. It is the time where the two kinds of citizens are mixed together, both in the church and in the nation. It is the time we have been allotted to bear this interwovenness in society and within ourselves—and to reorder our loves, making us fit to become heavenly citizens. Each individual is torn between the two cities and daily must renew her loyalty. This provides a chastened, self-critical edge to Augustine's view of education and citizenship. In his reading of pagan literature, there are bright moments of self-transcendence for the common good to be found and imitated even in pagan history (see Regulus in *CG* 5.24). There is also the possibility that we can delude ourselves and become even more prideful through the reading of Scripture, as Augustine says is the case with the Pelagian doctrine of Christian perfection.

For Augustine all of these distinctions—the enemy and friend, the prideful and humble, the lovers of God and the lovers of self, the two kinds of citizens, and the two cities and our judgments about them—are always provisional from the human point of view. They are provisional because the inhabitants of the two cities, the ultimately prideful and humble, are intermingled in this present age. They are provisional because we are always already dual citizens; our ultimate citizenship and our provisional citizenship (as in citizens of the United States of America or some other political body).

The secular names the time in which the two citizenries are mixed, in which we grapple with the text of Scripture and read it with and against the texts of human civilization. The city of God project is the project of education for citizenship in the secular age. Here we try to bring the wisdom of the records of human civilization and its vision of good citizens and a good society and hold them up to the light of

Scripture: analyzing, comparing, and contrasting how these visions hold up with what we know of membership in the heavenly city. To be an Augustinian reader of Scripture is to read and to be read by the Bible. It is to treat the Bible as the book of books with the most authoritative power for producing self-understanding and transformation. It is to read the Bible as *pilgrims* on the way to the heavenly city, within the horizon of the rule of faith (the basic tenets of orthodox Christian faith) and the ethical lens of the double commandments of love, and only secondarily as a historical artifact to be dissected or great work of literature to be debated. More than amassing information about the heavenly city, true reading of Scripture allows one entrance into that city's happiness as one learns to insert oneself into the narrative of Scripture.

There is fluidity between the texts of Scripture and the secular texts of the past, just as there is a fluid boundary between our present institutions and our ultimate destinations. If the first result of living in the *saeculum* is that we live provisional lives, the second is that we live textual lives. So much of becoming good citizens has to do with becoming good readers: those who inhabit great books and whose identities and loves are formed through the imaginative reception of inherited visions of the good life and good society.

Ultimately, we are citizens of a republic of letters, both temporal and eternal, both pagan and Christian. The city of God project is unending—which means that our commitments to education and the formation of good citizens can never be foreclosed, never too hastily identified with a temporal political community. Nor can any given political reality be too hastily rejected. For Augustine, the challenge in writing *The City of God* was to read the cultural memory of Ancient Rome (and by inheritance also the memory of Greece, Babylon, and Egypt) within the wisdom of God divinely inscribed in Scripture. The challenge of writing *The City of God* today would be to narrate the fruitful interaction of Athens, Jerusalem, and Rome in the formation of European and American Civilization—in Paris, London, and Philadelphia—as further expressions of this mixture of the two cities, an inheritance to be received with critical gratitude, and now extended to the frontiers of our increasingly global sense of civilizations. Education and citizenship require a deeply Augustinian sense of history. Augustine views human history as standing under the guidance of divine providence and divine judgment which means that we can resist—we must resist—both progressive and declension narratives about the present age. Things are always better than they could be and not yet as good as they should be. To live in a secular age and to educate good citizens in a secular society is to never quite know where we are in history. Without the narrative arc of history found in Scripture, one would have no way of naming ultimate progress or decline and because of this one can never name or define a precise location in history.

Dual citizenship

For Augustine, there are ultimately only two cities and two kinds of citizens. But in a second sense we are all always already dual citizens: citizens of a temporal political community and of an ultimate eschatological reality in which we mysteriously already participate by anticipation. Transcendence beyond the purely temporal or worldly realm gives education—and its fulfillment in the Augustinian purposes of contemplation and citizenship—an unlimited horizon, which opens the windows to the divine, releasing us from the pressures of our purely worldly ambitions and fears. Education and citizenship aimed purely at the instrumental ends of career achievement or riches will result either in narrowed nationalism and patriotic provincialism or a global, cosmopolitan utopia. Neither is adequate to our shared need for the spiritual community that fulfills and transcends our material bonds. So much of our current political hysteria and gnashing of teeth result from our limited horizon—our lack of hope for anything beyond material well-being. The Augustinian hope takes on a thoroughly Christ-centered expectation—a longing hope for "true justice [that] does not exist other than in that commonwealth whose Founder and Ruler is Christ" (*CG* 2.21).

This "other city" and other kind of citizenship that should guide Christian liberal arts education, for Augustine, allows one to form a healthy, limited loyalty and identification with one's political community and tradition—whether as Roman or American—and yet also provides a new understanding of global cosmopolitanism and global citizenship in the eternal city. We can be dual citizens, free to gratefully and critically appreciate our cultural inheritance while also keeping our critical edge and distance from any story that masquerades as the ultimate story about human nature and the goal of human history. The universal conception of "humanity"—and the fellow-feeling and identification with all other human beings that it denotes—flowers in the new form of limited politics found in the Christian community. The church, in Augustine's eyes, should strive to become the site of achievement for true diversity, meted out through love of both neighbor and enemy—as a signal to the political community in which it finds itself of the heavenly city's reality.

For Augustine, human difference always appears within the socially, linguistically, and historically coded expressions of strength over weakness, rightness, and wrongness, as well as the injustice that emerges from the messiness of human history. The sin, injustice, and domination that Augustine finds in history and in his own society are real and yet so too are the visions of unity-beyond-division found in Scripture's depiction of the heavenly city. This kind of communion, for Augustine, can only come as a result of recognizing our common humanity and weakness.

Although the church and the heavenly city are not synonymous or identical—and there is always an eschatological distance between the visible church and the invisible city of God—the church should strive, in Augustine's eyes, to become a site of prepolitical communion with other human beings in spite of cultural, linguistic, or historical difference and distance. The body of Christ, the church, becomes a place where overcoming difference happens through the recognition of true diversity.

> Therefore as long as this Heavenly City is a pilgrim on earth, she summons citizens of all nations and every tongue, and brings together a society of pilgrims in which no attention is paid to any differences in the customs, laws, and institutions by which earthly peace is achieved or maintained. She does not rescind or destroy these things, however. For whatever differences there are among the various nations, these all tend towards the same end of earthly peace. Thus, she preserves and follows them, provided only that they do not impede the religion by which we are taught that the one supreme and true God is to be worshipped. And so even the Heavenly City makes use of earthly peace during her pilgrimage, and desires and maintains the co-operation of men's wills in attaining those things which belong to the mortal nature of man, in so far as this may be allowed without prejudice to true godliness and religion. Indeed, she directs that earthly peace towards heavenly peace: towards the peace which is so truly such that—at least so far as rational creatures are concerned—only it can really be held to be peace and called such. For this peace is a perfectly ordered and perfectly harmonious fellowship in the enjoyment of God, and of one another in God. (*CG* 19.17)

The "earthly peace" of which Augustine speaks in this passage is that temporal happiness and civic well-being that comes through proper ordering of the temporal goods that make the concentric circles of friendship possible, as we saw in Chapter 2. Dual citizens ought to be committed to working for the achievement of this earthly peace by making proper "use" of it—that is, by referring this kind of social harmony toward its transcendent end in love for God and neighbor.

A liberal arts education is one of the chief temporal goods constitutive of earthly peace, in Augustine's eyes. The question becomes what does the referral and good use of this temporal good look like for us in the present age? At the most basic level it is the work of education that keeps the eternal city in view—a kind of liberal arts education that enacts the City of God project and cultivates love of God and neighbor as the intellectual and civic culmination of true education. Given the interwovenness of the two cities in time, our perspective of the liberal arts should tack back and forth between temporal, immediate aims and eternal, longer-range goods. Referring our use of a liberal arts education toward its true end in God means keeping the merely instrumental and economic aims of education wedded to the intrinsic purposes—cultivating a taste for justice as much as wealth, and wonder as much as intellectual mastery. One must first be thoroughly acquainted with the true vision of human well-being found in the heavenly city—glimpsed in the signs of Scripture and the Incarnation of Christ—and refer the use of the goods of liberal arts education toward that true end. Dual citizens are politically engaged—looking out for the temporal happiness of the political community through education, even as they are restlessly concerned for its eternal well-being.

Christian liberal arts education—and the Augustinian Christian liberal arts college—is the mode and institution by which dual citizens can be properly formed and trained to care for earthly peace and to perform the peculiarly dual-citizen work of redirecting all of this earthly peace (and all of its institutional goods) toward its true end in heavenly peace. In this way, the Augustinian Christian liberal arts college and its curriculum form a temporal institution that will dissolve when the pilgrimage is over, when there is no longer any need for referral or good use. But the institution will have served its purpose if it taught its students about the other city—and it is a purpose unlike any other institution in time, including the church.

5

A Way Forward

Introduction

The Augustinian vision balances the four goals of liberal arts education: intellectual, economic, moral, and spiritual. Each goal has its own question: What should I know? What will I make? What should I do? Who or what should I worship? The core purpose—the intellectual—must be simultaneously oriented toward the economic and practical on one side and the moral and spiritual on the other. It's a delicate balance that requires active attention and commitment. Indeed, the sea change currently under way in higher education derives from the loss of a common language for the moral and spiritual purposes of learning and an excessively instrumental—that is, economic—view of the value of a liberal arts college education. But, as noted in Chapter 1, to say that the moral and spiritual purposes of learning are lost is slightly misleading insofar as there must always be some guiding moral and spiritual purposes for the intellectual enterprise of education even if they remain inexplicit, unstated, or unexamined. In the present case, the economic purpose has filled the empty space of the previous models of the moral and spiritual purposes of learning, highlighting our increasingly materialist conceptions of the human person and human values.

Augustine's view of the moral and spiritual purposes of learning is a Christian adaptation of the Platonic view. The Platonic view holds that the moral purpose of a liberal arts education is the virtue of justice and good citizenship on the one hand and the spiritual purpose of divine contemplation on the other. Augustine reworks this dual-*telos* through the lens of the double commandments of love found in Scripture. This view of education includes an understanding of moral and spiritual formation, or properly ordered love. Ordered love within the context of liberal arts education moves in three directions. First is the inward ordering of the soul that happens as one acquires the moral and intellectual virtues necessary for disciplined study. Second is the upward ordering of love for God—a fulfillment of the command to love God with one's whole mind. Third is the outward ordering of affection for other human beings and one's sense of ethical responsibility to use education in service of humanity.

One of the essential catalysts for this kind of formation in liberal education, in Augustine's view, is the simple act of reading and discussing important books in a community of fellow learners. The intellectual skills cultivated and the context created for moral and spiritual transformation in this arrangement are profound. The content of such a reading plan is a great conversation between Scripture and other great works of Western civilization. Augustine narrates his conversion in *Confessions* as an example of this kind of reading.

To read the great books in a community of fellow learners is to participate in a critical dialogue between the divine wisdom found in Scripture and the human wisdom discerned in the records of human civilization. It is to participate in Augustine's "City of God Project." For Augustine, learning about the world is ultimately learning about one thing: God. Human history is the story of two cities—two ultimate societies that will be judged on the basis of their interior dispositions: love (healthy love for God and neighbor or excessive self-love), or pride and humility. To read world literature as the story of two cities is to be trained in the "two cities hermeneutic." The essential interpretive rubric for this hermeneutic is expressed in a personal, moral question that can only be asked by direct readers: "What affection does this text

stir in me?" This vision of reading and moral formation opens the way
to an alternate and ultimate sense of heavenly citizenship that stands
over any temporal political loyalty. By extension, it subordinates the
connection between liberal arts education and temporal citizenship
to a penultimate position.

With the theoretical lines of Augustine's view of liberal education
now in plain view, the question for inquisitive readers turns to the
practical: What would this picture look like in a liberal arts college
today? Here are three practical, essential features of the Augustinian
vision in action: a great books core curriculum, teacher training,
and patronage. Pursued together, these features would immediately
inspire the Augustinian vision within a liberal arts institution.

A great books core curriculum

The idea of a reinvigorating liberal arts education by introducing a
"great books" core curriculum has a long, rich heritage in the United
States. The great books movement of the early twentieth century—
forged at Columbia University under the guidance of John Erskine
and Mortimer Adler, and Robert Maynard Hutchins at the University
of Chicago, among others—was premised on the simple idea that
core courses should be taught by a pair of instructors who read one
important book each week and spend a few hours discussing it with a
small group of students. Although there were many variations on the
texts required from the canon of great works in the arts, humanities,
and social and natural sciences—as well as variation in the adjacent
requirements of essay writing and comprehensive examination—the
basic blueprint remained consistent: a great books reading list and
Socratic seminar pedagogy (where instructors are trained in guiding
discussion by asking questions). This model was central not only
to the core curriculum reforms at Columbia and the University of

Chicago but also to the birth of many great books programs in the mid-twentieth century, such as Notre Dame's Program in Liberal Studies. Then it developed entire great books colleges, such as the one at St. John's, and many more offshoots of one-year great texts sequences at institutions like Reed College and St. Olaf College.

More recently, the late twentieth and early twenty-first centuries witnessed many religious liberal arts institutions picking up the great books baton. Zaytuna, for example—a Muslim liberal arts college in Berkeley, California—houses a great books core curriculum in the Islamic tradition. And many great books honors programs in Christian liberal arts institutions have emerged, such as Torrey Honors Institute at Biola University and Baylor University's Honors College. Because many of the programs at Christian liberal arts institutions are forthrightly Christian and include large doses of Scripture and open conversation between Christian faith and the ideas developed in the great texts of Western civilization, they often become Augustinian in outlook by default. This happens not only because students are exposed to Augustine's works and immediately sense his influence in the West, but because the very idea of a Christian great books program is Augustine's invention in the *Confessions* and *City of God*, and students and faculty intuitively recognize this. This intuition should be made fully explicit and worked into the whole of the curriculum (which extends far beyond Augustine's particular historical vantage) and practiced at the level of moral and spiritual formation.

Chronology

A distinctively Augustinian approach to a great books core curriculum is both Socratic (the art of Socrates' open-ended questioning of terms and definitions) and Christ-centered (committed to the spiritual authority of Christ, the teacher of true wisdom). The curriculum hosts the critical dialogue between pagan wisdom and Scripture.

An Augustinian Christian understanding of history—and the meta-narrative of creation, fall, redemption, and eschaton—requires that the curriculum be studied in chronological sequence.

By taking this historical point of view, an Augustinian core curriculum gains internal resources to resist a triumphalist narrative of the canon of great works of Western civilization on the one hand and skeptical alienation and deconstruction of the Western tradition on the other. The Augustinian approach does not see the canon as a representative set of texts that bear witness to the spirit of the age or the rational unfolding of human freedom. Instead, the canon is a provisional attempt to tell the Christian story of the search for God and God's search for humankind—the story of the two cities. Because history is ultimately the story of God's pilgrim city, the texts that count as part of this story always respond to the movement of God's Spirit in the church today, far beyond the frontiers of Western civilization.

A forward-looking and hopeful curriculum also avoids the pitfall of being overly wedded to the past in a kind of nostalgic, intellectual idolatry. Its content spans the entire timeline of human discourse, always sure to carry students' dialogue with great texts all the way up to the present moment in appreciation of the contemporary authors, thinkers, and creators puzzling over the big questions: What is the happy life? What is the good society? It's a curriculum that inquires about the present as much as it does about the past: Who are the Homers and Augustines today? By remaining *hopeful* in the Christian sense, the curriculum unfolds the present moment as a stimulating challenge for synthesis, because Jesus Christ is the Lord of History and the movement of time is the story of the pilgrim city.

Constrained agreement

If the content of the curriculum is the critical dialogue between Scripture and pagan wisdom—and the ongoing manifestation of that dialogue in the great works of Christian civilization such as Dante's *Divine Comedy* or Milton's *Paradise Lost*—the method of classroom dialogue is both Socratic and tradition-shaped, as with Alasdair MacIntyre's sense of constrained agreement and disagreement. Scripture is approached therefore both as one of the world's great texts and as the divinely authoritative book of books. This model is an invitation to further questioning and reverent appreciation of the truthfulness of Scripture. Constrained agreement, which makes genuine disagreement possible, often begins in the form of an institution's faith and lifestyle statement that articulates the basic tenets of Christian belief and practice required for membership in the learning community. Yet, the context of faith seeking true understanding allows room for debate, doubt, and questioning—so that students can move toward understanding, and perhaps toward faith, through struggle in periods of unknowing. This prolonged process often peels back the forms of false certainty and intellectual idolatry that have corroded authentic faith—just as Skepticism and Neoplatonism did for Augustine in his movement from Manichaeism to authentic Christian faith.

Seminar instructors bring their own faithful intellectual searching to the seminar table, helping students overcome the compartmentalization of faith in modern society and providing them with a critical vision of faith in its wholeness. This helps students to not outgrow the Christian faith of their childhood or, if they don't have faith, to not remain stuck with a childhood understanding of what Christian faith amounts to. In the Augustinian view, the church remains a central place for Christian teaching and formation, yet the church cannot be expected to make the wide-ranging connections of Christian faith to all areas of learning that the Christian college can. Nor can it be expected to provide the context or staff to nurture the far-reaching questions and intellectual discovery that is the special province of a Christian liberal arts college.

Predisciplinary learning

The best great books core curricula are those that enliven the conversation between Scripture, Christian thought and pagan wisdom, while integrating the greatest number of disciplines possible into their history of ideas—including the history of math, science, art, music, etc. Texts from nonliterary disciplines often require their own approaches of interpretation and discussion and take the traditional "great books" teacher—usually from the humanities—beyond her depth and expertise. This is a worthy and important challenge, and the best programs offer a fully integrated approach to the history of ideas. Indeed, most of the texts in a great books core curriculum are themselves "predisciplinary" and don't neatly fall into any specialized field of study—or at least not by the author's intent—but have been categorized and isolated by the modern approach to liberal arts education.

Expertise has been so thoroughly expanded and developed today that the university's disciplines are often very fragmented. Even in the humanities, it is intimidating to talk to a professor from another field, not to mention someone from the natural or social sciences. To overcome this barrier to multidimensional learning, the best core curricula model a predisciplinary dialogue for students. It begins with training teachers to speak across the lines of traditional disciplines and supporting them to write their scholarly work in this mode. These curricula may also include hosted, on-campus dialogues that showcase a predisciplinary approach to the big questions pressing upon students and culture—for example, questions about evolutionary theory and divine creation, sexuality and behavioral psychology, politics and human nature, and so on. The great books core becomes not only a curriculum with undergraduate seminars but a laboratory for predisciplinary learning and conversation—the space for human beings who love learning to pursue knowledge together. The curriculum forms a community of educators who can experimentally engage big ideas and make vulnerable attempts at communicating them to nonspecialists in the broader community.

An Augustinian great texts core curriculum gives every student—including those in STEM subjects and professional majors, such as nursing and engineering—a way into the richness of the liberal arts tradition that is meaningful, integrated, and connected to faith. It charts the way toward integration rather than fragmentation, and formation rather than information.

A small, nimble curriculum that fits with all the majors and disciplines within the institution allows for maximal cohesion and testifies to the importance of the four purposes of liberal learning—intellectual, moral, spiritual, and economic. Such a great books core curriculum need not pretend to cover everything and leaves room for discipline-specific study of the quantitative fields not adequately approached from a great texts point of view.

Studies indicate that the more coherent and uniform a core sequence is across the four-year college curriculum, the more likely it is to nurture outside-the-classroom discussion and to inspire the forms of intellectual and spiritual friendship central to generating a stimulating learning community. In the final year of such a sequence, a capstone intellectual project ties the great dialogue and the wisdom of the ages to a question relevant in one's field of study. For example, a premed student could write a thesis on the meaning of human suffering that discusses Greek tragedy, Simone Weil, and pain medication abuse.

A core curriculum and community of learning defined along these lines could save the liberal arts college as it seeks to broaden its reach by engaging its community in ways relevant to the daily lives of citizens. In this model, the conference table is a place of experimentation and hypothesis, where intellectual breakthroughs are the reward of interactive dialogue, self-examination, and cultural engagement. Yet, repeated attempts to make the great books-related disciplines model themselves on the results-driven research agendas of the natural and social sciences have only created further distance from the object of their pursuit: true human wisdom. Wisdom is vulnerable, requires time, and guarantees no material reward. At the same time, if great books education becomes defensive—a faith-afraid environment where everything must be defended beforehand—generative risk-taking, the hallmark of the sciences, will disappear from dialogue around the conference room table. An overly mechanized approach to the human sciences kills the creativity, vulnerability, and intuition required to make progress in the pursuit of wisdom.

The value of an Augustinian great books core curriculum

Although the Augustinian model is not "cheap" in financial terms, it is also not expensive in terms of resources: One only needs a room, table, chairs, books, and people to engage in constructive dialogue. It is a very cost-effective model if one takes into view statistics of student recruitment, retention, skills development, moral formation, performance within one's major, student leadership formation, etc. that often result from a coherent core curriculum. The past century in higher education in the United States suggests that there is often a significant benefit in terms of recruitment numbers and student quality that immediately ensues when a school implements a great books curriculum. It gives the school an intellectual identity—an identity that each student, regardless of major or extracurricular interests, has in common—and becomes part of the shared, long-term loyalty of the students to the institutions.

Prospective students and their families can be told in one or two sentences what the difference is between going to college and a trade school, between a smorgasbord of disconnected introductory classes in the disciplinary model of general education that is found in most universities and the rich, coherent feast of a great books core curriculum. The core curriculum wars over the past century are the product of the disciplinary imagination. They are turf wars that do not benefit students. What is needed is a return to a simple vision—a simple curriculum, a simple pedagogical model, and a simple view of the moral and spiritual formation that complements the intellectual and economic purposes of learning.

The great books movement of the early twentieth century—the one started in Columbia's Common Core and that has transformed many elite colleges and universities into what they are today—was premised on the simple idea that some books merit reading more than others, and that educated citizens should spend at least part of their time in college meditating on and discussing these works. How much more so do Christians—the inheritors of the Bible and the masterwork *The City of God*—have a stake in bringing students into this conversation as the bedrock of their liberal arts experience, the lasting foundation of their Christian faith, and the tools to bring faith into conversation in the present age? The Augustinian vision is perhaps the most persuasive and morally and spiritually charged vision for installing a great books core curriculum as the bedrock of a liberal arts education.

Teacher training

For an Augustinian great books curriculum to be successful, it needs good teachers who are trained in four essential tasks—purveying the history of ideas, Socratic seminar pedagogy, the ability to write persuasively for nonspecialists, and moral and spiritual formation. Building and supporting a cadre of teachers equipped for these four tasks is a central responsibility for an Augustinian liberal arts institution. Depending on the institution's size and budget (and disciplinary model of departments), it can be effective to hire and train a team of teachers who are singularly devoted to the task of teaching and mentoring students in the core curriculum.

The history of ideas

Currently, there are no formal training environments for teachers of great books curricula. The traditional humanities research model of dissertation and specialized disciplinary research—and the ongoing formation of guild associations, conferences, journals, and publications—is insufficient on its own for forming teachers who are conversant in the history of ideas, or "The City of God Project," in the Augustinian context. Indeed, the traditional training of doctoral programs is an essential gateway into a great books core curriculum, but it must be supplemented by initiation into the critical dialogue of Scripture and the canon of great works—a conversation where teachers hone the predisciplinary language they need for teaching undergraduates in an Augustinian great books core curriculum. An institute devoted to such training would be much like a great books curriculum for teachers—a place where teachers experience the great conversation themselves as a way of preparing to take students along for the adventure.

Socratic pedagogy

To be an inspiring teacher in an Augustinian great books curriculum is to be an inspired participant in the great conversation. It is to be a fellow learner who has a large intellectual appetite and can entertain wide-ranging questions about texts that connect with questions of human value and significance. Being trained for this kind of work first requires one to study with great teachers, both living and dead, and to imitate such exemplars.

Socratic pedagogy is primarily the art of asking good questions—
questions that are not too leading or open-ended. Learning to ask
questions that bring students into the very heart of the text without
overwhelming the group's energy or the individual student's ownership
of the discussion is difficult and requires thorough training. Given
that many of the big questions of significance and value found in the
great works require a lifetime of discovery and a life lived to answer, it
is the method most suited to the subject matter.

Today one can hear or watch lectures on Shakespeare by the
greatest experts at Stanford or Harvard for free online, but she'll have a
hard time finding face-to-face conversations about what Shakespeare
means, where she can insert her own voice into the conversation in
that forum. A great books core curriculum is about the face-to-face,
the particular, the personal, and the relational—it forms a community
that holds itself accountable for the conversation it keeps.

Writing and publication

Given the distinctiveness of this approach to the history of ideas and
Socratic seminar pedagogy itself, the standard academic practices
of research, writing, and publication demanded of teachers may
become unsustainable amidst the work of teaching in the curriculum.
Emphasizing communication that resembles the great conversation—
literature written for undergraduate-level readers and a broader
popular audience—redoubles the spirit and intent of the curriculum,
and models the intellectual virtues that could otherwise remain
theoretical in the gap between ideas and action. This kind of writing
production could inspire and invite those outside elite scholarly circles
into the riches of the history of ideas. The intellectual community
of Christian liberal arts colleges needs a teacher-evaluation model
that reforms the last century's turn toward a scientific rubric for
the humanities—one built to recognize and reward teachers who

can communicate in the mode of predisciplinary conversation. Success is student-centric: Teachers who can do more than express the scholarly ins and outs of books and historical contexts—who can make plain the richness of texts for the human tasks of living, loving and finding meaning—earn the highest praise. This model of writing and publication should not be seen as an easy way out but rather as a profoundly difficult challenge. To write in the manner of the current research model on topics related to the great books is to write like a footnote machine that reduces its subject to the status of the object in the natural and social sciences. Much more demanding and difficult would be to write in a way suited to the subject matter—to write in a form that matches or aspires to the level of originality, creativity, and power of the books that are under consideration.

Formation

Teachers who teach in the great books core curriculum should be specially trained—not just in terms of the history of ideas, Socratic seminar pedagogy, and in communicating with a wider audience, but in the art of fully inhabiting the intellectual story of the Augustinian great books sequence. They should be specially equipped to care for students' moral and spiritual lives at the intersection of the intellectual, economic, moral, and spiritual purposes of learning. By their ability to articulate the intellectual story, and to think through questions, and also by their exemplarity and witness, these teachers foster the inward, upward, and outward movements of ordered love in students as mentors and guides.

Teachers in the great books common core are the priests of an Augustinian liberal arts college. Although there's an important role for the ritual life of worship and reflection on Scripture, in the unique season of formation and instruction that happens in undergraduate study, it is the questions and conversations that naturally emerge from *the great dialogue* in the core that stirs up the richest, most pressing and intense questions that need thoughtful and mature Christian reflection. The college does not replace the church and teachers are encouraged to be active in the life of a local congregation, supporting a complementary vision of the intellectual role of the college and the pastoral role of the church.

Training for teaching in a great books curriculum ought to be as intense as the initiation of a traditional doctoral program, and the ongoing standards of excellence for publication ought to be as high as many of the publication standards in scholarly guilds and disciplinary associations. Teacher training should look to the most rigorous and demanding vocations for inspiration and guidance—for example, Navy Seals, Jesuits, professional athletics—where a sense of identity and purpose provide a strong team spirit and where the results of a shared effort are judged on the basis of the whole community's performance.

In this environment, a hypothetical college president asks a wholly different set of questions, for example: Can a teacher write in a way that inspires and invites a broader audience—in a way that imitates or even matches the power of the great books themselves? Can a teacher teach in a way that challenges and transforms students—not only intellectually but also morally and spiritually? Can a teacher live a life that is an exemplary witness of the truthfulness of the ideas under consideration?

Currently, there are no graduate programs where teachers can be trained in the four tasks of the history of ideas, seminar pedagogy, the ability to write persuasively for nonspecialists, and moral and spiritual formation. A short-term solution would be to create postdoctoral programs associated with great books core curricula that train recent PhDs headed toward teaching in liberal arts colleges in the four tasks. A program of this kind would serve as a creative center for graduate students who are ready to think about education in the broadest sense—ready to take risks, make connections far outside their fields of expertise, and to experiment in the laboratory of learning. The program's catalytic effect—or what seasoned professors often refer to as its therapy—would stem from the way a great books core curriculum can help revivify one's reasons for pursuing teaching in the first place. For teachers in the undergraduate core, a PhD is a rite of passage but not a way of life.

In the present moment, the best teachers have little incentive to teach in the fields related to a great books core curriculum. The combination of a PhD in a specialized field of study compounded with the prospect of making $50,000 a year or less after a decade of preparation scares away many of the people that should be teaching in such programs. Incentivizing teachers with lucrative salaries is obviously not the complete answer—indeed, it would be an ironic turn back to the purely economic end. Yet the decision to compensate teachers in a more commensurate and representative fashion would imply that institutions have asked themselves if they should pay healthier salaries to skilled faculty. One prevailing alternative is to farm out the majority of core curriculum classes—especially in the humanities—to highly overworked and underpaid adjunct faculty. It's a striking maneuver in short-term expediency that sacrifices strategic, long-term institutional vitality. We should not underestimate what people can do if they feel supported in their endeavors and, moreover, what the alleged value of their labor deserves.

Getting traction in any of these four tasks requires a long duration of education and formation. And the training required to become a good teacher in the Augustinian core curriculum is not immediately productive in financial terms. Thus, because the runway to a life in teaching begins early, students in liberal arts colleges need to hear a positive message about the viability of education as a profession. In brief, students need not choose between an instrumental, economic understanding of their college experience and the pursuit of an intellectual life ordered to the moral and spiritual purposes of learning. Formation can be a both/and dynamic—a process that both enriches the mind and prepares the hands, as it were. Indeed, the rise of applied sciences and professional majors within liberal arts colleges makes this dream a reality—as long as administrators and leaders are brave enough to hold the four purposes of learning together, and patrons are generous enough to support such visions. The first and most strategic move a patron interested in supporting liberal education might make is to support talented individuals to be trained in the fourfold tasks of an Augustinian great books core curriculum.

Patronage

An education in the liberal arts is a gift or privilege that presumes one has secured the leisure, as classical authors call it, to spend four years away from the "productive" practices of career and profession. Costly and all-consuming, it requires strong support from a sympathetic, believing community. That is, it requires patronage.

Augustine's story spotlights the importance of patronage for liberal education. His early career as a teacher in North Africa and Italy was made possible by a local patron named Romanianus. Later, his experiment in Christian liberal education at Cassiciacum was made possible by the use of the villa owned by a rich friend, named Verecundus. After Cassiciacum, patronage made Augustine's Christian liberal arts commune in North Africa possible. The list goes on. For without the gifts and resources of the wealthy and generous, there is simply no way to create the time and space for student learning along the lines of an Augustinian model—with historical perspective, moral depth, and spiritual insight for the present age. It is a deep and demanding formation that does not immediately produce marketable goods. Generous gifts have always been the economic basis of an excellent liberal arts education—from the ancient world to the present.

The only way to overcome the soaring costs of higher education without continuing to solely rely on family pocketbooks and government aid is to inspire a new generation of donors who believe in the intrinsic moral and spiritual purposes of learning and the value of student soul formation. The overwhelming success of the empirical sciences and technology—both in university research and in the economy—threatens to limit the discerning patron's imagination of the soul work of forming good human beings through liberal education. Liberal education's champions are often—like clergy— not financially equipped to sustain the vision to which their lives are committed. Complex as the reasons for this may be, the need for patronage is clear: Those who've acquired surplus in life become critical partners in the future of liberal arts institutions and, by extension, in student lives. For Christians, the internal goods of soul formation are invaluable and eternal, which means patrons deserve true gratitude in return.

If a college and its benefactors invest in such a program, students will come. And they will not only learn how to get somewhere in the world, they will learn what kind of person they ought to be, and what they ought to do when they get there. The Augustinian vision opens the instrumental course of learning—from the intellectual to the economic—into an infinite horizon, where the soul stretches and a place opens for goods that transcend the visible world. A liberal arts education is a gift in every sense, in Augustine's eyes—from the time, resources, and attention of good teachers, to one's natural abilities and their development in the course of a life. A good education is as much given as it is achieved. Augustine once wrote to a man named Firmus who had inquired about Augustine's willingness to tutor his son: "His great gifts which are outstanding because of his great natural talent and highly developed through a liberal education have filled me with great joy. But you know very well that the *end* to which these goods are applied is of great importance" (*L* 2*). The *end* to which one puts a good education makes all the difference. Now is the time to renew the moral and spiritual purposes of learning, for without such an orientation the horizon of the liberal arts will narrow, making education not merely less divine, but less human.

Bibliography

Arum, Richard & Josipa Roksa, *Academically Adrift: Limited Learning on College Campuses* (Chicago, IL: University of Chicago, 2010).

Bloom, Allan, *The Closing of the American Mind: How Higher Education Has Failed Democracy and Impoverished the Souls of Today's Students* (New York: Simon & Schuster, 1987).

Brooks, David, *The Road to Character* (New York: Random House, 2015).

Deresiewicz, William, *Excellent Sheep: The Miseducation of the American Elite and the Way to a Meaningful Life* (New York: Free Press, 2014).

Emerson, Ralph Waldo, *The Essential Writings of Ralph Waldo Emerson*, ed. by Brooks Atkinson (New York: Modern Library, 2000).

Lewis, C.S., *The Weight of Glory and Other Addresses* (New York: Touchstone/Simon & Schuster, 1996).

MacIntyre, Alasdair, *Three Rival Versions of Moral Enquiry: Encyclopaedia, Genealogy, and Tradition* (Notre Dame, IN: University of Notre Dame Press, 1990),

Paffenroth, Kim & Kevin L. Hughes (eds.), *Augustine and Liberal Education* (Lanham, MD: Lexington Books, 2008).

Pollmann, Karla & Mark Vessey (eds.), *Augustine and the Disciplines: From Cassiciacum to Confessions* (New York: Oxford University Press, 2005).

Seneca, *Letters from a Stoic*, trans. Robin Campbell (New York: Penguin, 1969).

Stock, Brian, *Augustine the Reader: Meditation, Self-Knowledge, and the Ethics of Interpretation* (Cambridge, MA: Harvard University Press, 1998).

Thoreau, Henry David, *Walden* and *Resistance to Civil Government*, ed. by William Rossi (New York: Norton, 1992).

Topping, Ryan N.S., *Happiness and Wisdom: Augustine's Early Theology of Education* (Washington, DC: The Catholic University of America Press, 2012).

Topping, Ryan N.S., *St. Augustine*, Bloomsbury Library of Educational Thought (London: Bloomsbury, 2010).

Index